CHRISTIAN HEROES: THEN & NOW

GEORGE MÜLLER

The Guardian of Bristol's Orphans

Christian Heroes: Then & Now

GEORGE MÜLLER

The Guardian of Bristol's Orphans

JANET & GEOFF BENGE

YWAM Publishing is the publishing ministry of Youth With A Mission (YWAM), an international missionary organization of Christians from many denominations dedicated to presenting Jesus Christ to this generation. To this end, YWAM has focused its efforts in three main areas: (1) training and equipping believers for their part in fulfilling the Great Commission (Matthew 28:19), (2) personal evangelism, and (3) mercy ministry (medical and relief work).

To learn more about our books and materials, call (425) 771-1153 or (800) 922-2143 or email books@ywampublishing.com. Visit us online at www.ywampublishing.com.

George Müller: The Guardian of Bristol's Orphans

Published by YWAM Publishing
a ministry of Youth With A Mission
P.O. Box 55787, Seattle, WA 98155-0787

ISBN 978-1-57658-145-2 (paperback)
ISBN 978-1-57658-563-4 (e-book)

Twenty-second printing 2025

Printed in the United States of America

Christian Heroes: Then & Now

Adoniram Judson
Albert Schweitzer
Amy Carmichael
Betty Greene
Brother Andrew
Cameron Townsend
Charles Mulli
Clarence Jones
Corrie ten Boom
Count Zinzendorf
C. S. Lewis
C. T. Studd
David Bussau
David Livingstone
Dietrich Bonhoeffer
D. L. Moody
Elisabeth Elliot
Eric Liddell
Florence Young
Francis Asbury
George Müller
Gladys Aylward
Helen Roseveare
Hudson Taylor
Ida Scudder
Isobel Kuhn
Jacob DeShazer
Jim Elliot
John Flynn
John Newton
John Wesley
John Williams
Jonathan Goforth
Klaus-Dieter John
Lillian Trasher
Loren Cunningham
Lottie Moon
Mary Slessor
Mildred Cable
Nate Saint
Norman Grubb
Paul Brand
Rachel Saint
Richard Wurmbrand
Rowland Bingham
Samuel Zwemer
Sundar Singh
Wilfred Grenfell
William Booth
William Carey

Available in paperback, e-book, and audiobook formats. Unit study curriculum guides are available for select biographies.

www.YWAMpublishing.com

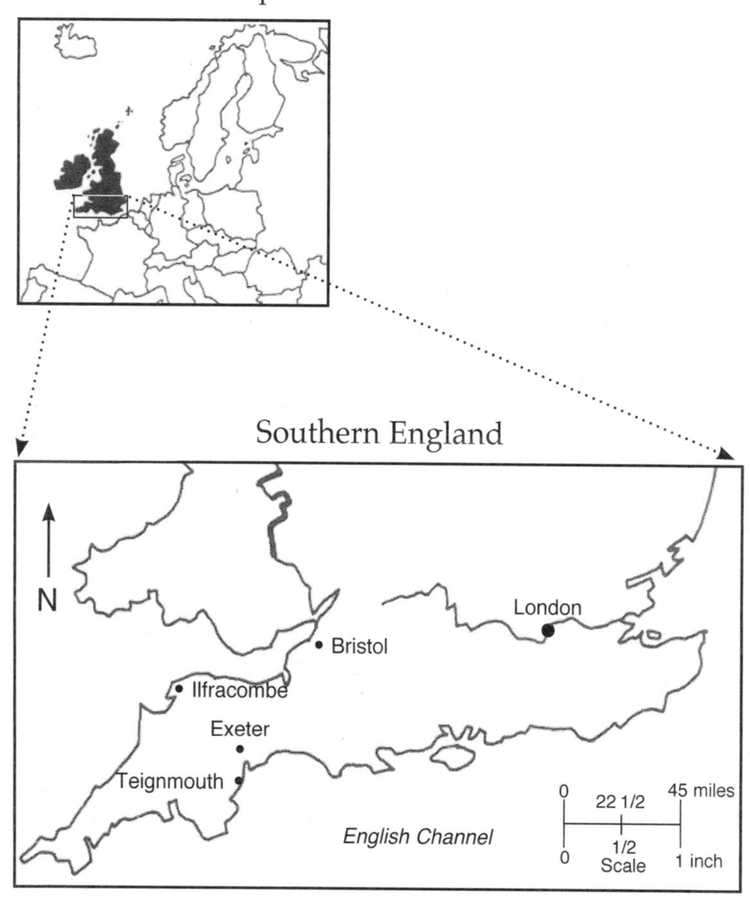

Northern Europe
Southern England
N
London
Bristol
Ilfracombe
Exeter
Teignmouth
English Channel
0
22 1/2
45 miles
0
1/2
Scale
1 inch

Contents

1. A Common Thief 11
2. The Life of the Party 25
3. Something Was Strangely Different 37
4. Too Childish for a Grown Man 49
5. A Free Man 63
6. A New Beginning 73
7. A Mission Field Right Here 85
8. The Breakfast Club 95
9. The First Orphanage in Bristol 109
10. An Orphanage on Wilson Street 119
11. Food for the Children 129
12. Do unto Others 141
13. Ashley Down 153
14. God Will Supply 165
15. Traveling Days 177
16. After Tomorrow 191
17. The Work Goes On 199

Bibliography 204

Chapter 1

A Common Thief

Crash! A flowerpot toppled over onto the sidewalk beneath George Müller as he stretched his foot out to reach the ground. George was climbing out the back window of the inn where he had been staying, and when he heard the crash, he froze. After he was satisfied no one had heard him, he lowered one foot softly onto the cobbled pavement, then the other. Sixteen-year-old George pulled his tall, lanky body up to its full height and looked around. "Good," he muttered to himself under his breath. "I'm safe. Now to get out of here."

A moment later George realized he'd spoken too soon. Police officers appeared at either end of the street and began running towards him. George swung around, desperately looking for some way to escape, but there was none. Before he knew it, the strong hands of a policeman had grabbed his arm and were dragging him roughly along the cobblestone street in the direction of the jail.

An hour later, George was waiting for his name to be called. The backless wooden bench he sat on was hard and uncomfortable, and the chains around his slender wrists and ankles bit at his flesh.

As he waited, George thought about how shocked his father would be to see him in shackles. Then again, his father probably wouldn't be any more shocked than George was right then. George had done dishonest things many times before, but this was the first time he'd been caught. That is, the first time he'd been caught by the police. When he was ten years old, he'd been caught by his father, and it turned out to be a painful and humiliating experience. His father, Johann Müller, was a tax collector for the Prussian government, and he often left large sums of money in the house. Mr. Müller often complained that small amounts of this money were missing, but George, like his younger brother, passionately declared he knew nothing about it.

One day George was called into his father's office, where his father had laid a trap for him. Mr. Müller had counted out a number of coins and left them on the corner of his desk. When George arrived at the office, his father pretended he needed to go into another room. Alone in the office, George saw the pile of coins on his father's desk and thought of all the wonderful things he could do with the money. It seemed such a shame to put all of the coins into the official black leather pouch his father used for collecting tax money and hand the money over to some government official. So George crept up to the desk and quietly lifted three coins from the top of the pile. Who would miss them? George quickly dropped the coins inside his right sock.

When Johann Müller returned to the office, much to George's dismay, he looked straight at the pile of coins. "How strange," he said in a low, constrained voice George had come to fear. "I thought there were more coins there than that. Let me count them."

George could feel his cheeks becoming hot and flushed. His heart began to race. The cold coins pressed against his ankle inside his sock.

"Empty your pockets," said Mr. Müller evenly, looking his son in the eye.

"But Papa…," George began and then thought better of it. Obediently, he emptied his pockets onto the desk. There were a quill nib, three glass marbles, and a foot-long piece of string. George turned his pockets inside out so that his father could see that they were empty.

"Now take off your shirt."

George was horrified. How far would his father go before he believed his oldest son?

"And your pants."

George began to fret. Things were not looking good. If his father found the coins in his sock, George would be beaten. And from previous experience,

George knew that a boy without his pants on made an especially good target.

"Now your socks," continued his father in a determined voice.

George inched them off his feet, first the left and then the right, being careful to gather the coins in such a way that they wouldn't clink together.

"Hand them over," demanded his father.

George's heart raced even faster. His face felt like it was on fire now. George lowered his eyes as he gave the socks to his father.

A second later his father exploded. "My son, a common thief! How dare you disgrace the name of Müller. Come here now." He reached for the cane that stood propped in the corner of his office.

Crack! Crack! Crack! The caning seemed to go on forever. The pain was excruciating. Eventually George felt his legs begin to buckle under him, just as his father's temper subsided and the punishment came to an end.

"Don't ever steal again. Do you hear?" said Johann Müller, shaking his son's shoulders to emphasize each word.

"Yes," stuttered George.

"Now get out of my sight," roared his father, pointing at the door.

George gathered his clothes and half walked, half crawled to the door, not even stopping to dress. Right then he didn't care who saw him; his bottom was throbbing too much. He made his way up to his second-floor bedroom, where he locked the door behind him. Safe inside, he collapsed onto the bed and began to sob his heart out. "As long as I live, I'll never do that again," he promised himself between sobs, at the same time running his fingers over the welts on his legs and buttocks.

George wasn't promising himself he wouldn't steal again. No, he loved the thrill and adventure of stealing too much for that, not to mention its rewards. What George Müller promised himself was that he would never get caught again. Stealing was exciting, but getting caught was painful and humiliating!

Now, six years later, he had allowed himself to get caught again. How could he have been so stupid? He asked himself the question over and over as he sat on the hard wooden bench in the police station.

"You!" a police officer said, pointing at George. "Come here, and hurry up about it."

"Yes, sir," George replied, getting to his feet as best he could with the chains wrapped around him. As he shuffled over to the desk, he held his head up high and tried to look like an obedient young man who had been wrongly accused.

"Name?" asked the police officer.

"Müller, sir, George Müller."

The police officer wrote it down in a huge leather-bound book. "Date and place of birth," he asked when he'd finished writing.

"September 27, 1805, in Kroppenstaedt, Prussia."

The police officer began writing in the book again, stopping only to redip his quill pen in a bottle of India ink. As he watched, George wondered how much the police actually knew. Did they know he had spent a week at an inn in Brunswick and left there without paying before coming to Wolfenbüttel?

If they didn't know, George determined to keep his wits about him and not give away any more information than he absolutely had to. After three hours of relentless questioning, though, he confessed to all his crimes. Yes, he had spent a week in an expensive inn at Brunswick and left without paying the bill. Yes, he was trying to do the same thing in Wolfenbüttel by escaping through the window of the inn. No, he did not have the money to pay for the rooms. And no, he could not think of one good reason why he should not be sent to jail to await trial.

The next day, George sat in his cell humming a Christmas carol. It was Christmas Day, but what did that matter now? George had spent the previous five Christmases at the Cathedral Classical School at Halberstadt, where he had studied Latin, French, the German classics, and arithmetic. Everything had been so simple there; his teachers were easy to fool. From the time he was twelve he'd been able to escape school at night and go to beer-drinking parties, card games, and local entertainment houses to play the piano and the guitar. After graduating, instead of going home, George had decided to take a short trip. And that's how his present troubles had started. He had written his father that he'd been asked to stay two weeks longer at school to sing at a special church service. Then he had hit the road without any money to tour Lower Saxony, which in turn had landed him in jail.

How could he have been so stupid? He had plenty of time to think about the answer. Days went by, and the only thing he had to look forward to was the black bread and salty vegetable gruel he was fed twice a day. By the time he'd been in the cell a week, he knew every inch of it, from the initials T. W. carved in the stone above his bed to the groove in the wall that ran parallel with the bars in the window to the nail on the middle hinge of the thick wooden door that was shinier than the others. George also wondered whether his father had received a letter from the authorities informing him where his son was.

George kept count of the days he'd spent in jail by scratching a mark on the wall each time the early morning sunlight crept through the cell window. It was January 16. He had now been imprisoned for twenty-four days. For all he knew, he could be there for another twenty-four, or even two hundred twenty-four, days. At midmorning, he heard a promising sound. Keys jangled in the lock, and his cell door creaked open. Two policemen walked in and yanked George to his feet.

"Your father has come to get you out, but I wouldn't say you're free!"

As the policeman laughed at his own joke, George groaned. His father would be in a terrible mood. And he was. He paid George's debt to the two innkeepers and another sum to cover the cost of George's keep while in jail. George was then released into his father's care.

As father and son climbed into a horse-drawn coach for the journey home, Johann Müller hissed at George. "What would your mother think of her oldest son? Answer me that." For the rest of the trip he sat in stony silence.

George couldn't answer the question. His mother had died suddenly two years before, but he'd been so busy with his friends he hardly missed her. He wished he felt bad about disappointing her—and disappointing his father—but he didn't. He was just sorry he'd been caught. He was also sorry about what was going to happen when they arrived home!

After traveling all day, the coach pulled to a halt in front of the Müller home. George climbed out, trying to control his trembling hands. As he walked inside, his father pointed towards his office. George's shoulders slumped. George had expected the worst, and sure enough, he received the longest and harshest beating he had ever endured. It was days before he could walk properly again.

About a week later, Johann Müller called his son into his office and told him it was time to grow up and make something of himself. To that end he had enrolled George in the University of Halle. George's heart skipped a beat. That was exactly where he'd dreamed of going! But his father was not finished. Yes, George would be going to Halle, one of the best universities in Europe, to study the classics, but his father had arranged for him to have a personal tutor while he was there. This tutor, whom Mr. Müller had already selected, would stick to George like glue. George would report to him before and after all his classes. And the tutor would study with George each evening and on the weekends. He would also send a weekly report home on George's progress.

George could hardly believe it. A tutor! How could his father do that to him? It would be as bad as being in jail. All the other young men would be out enjoying themselves, and he would be stuck in his room studying. There had to be some way around it.

There was, but it involved a lot of lying and scheming. George decided it was unthinkable to go to the University of Halle with a personal tutor, so without his father's knowledge he made a secret trip to the town of Nordhausen, where he applied to a smaller pre-university school. Since he had always made good grades no matter how little he studied, he was quickly accepted into the school.

Then he began wondering how he would tell his father of his plans. Each night as he lay in bed, George promised himself that tomorrow would be the right time to break the news. But when tomorrow came, something always seemed to get in the way. The months rolled by. The morning of September 30 dawned, the day before George was due to leave for the University of Halle. George took a deep breath; it was now or never.

Johann Müller was furious when he heard the news. When would the lies end? How could George turn down an opportunity like Halle for some little pre-university school? The questions went on and on, but in the end, George's father could see it was no use. George was now seventeen years old and couldn't be made to study anywhere he did not want to. Reluctantly Johann Müller gave permission for his son to attend school at Nordhausen, pointing out that George was bound to regret his decision.

George Müller loved living in Nordhausen, one of the oldest cities in Prussia, tucked up against the edge of the lower slopes of the Harz Mountains. In his spare time, George liked nothing better than to walk through the town and into the beautiful valley below. But he did not have much spare time. He had promised himself he would study hard, and that's what he did. Most days he rose at four in the morning and did schoolwork all day until ten at night, when he fell into bed exhausted.

That was most of the time. Occasionally, though, he took a night off. And that's when he started to get into trouble. It was the gambling and partying again, two activities that cost a lot of money. His father provided him with a small allowance, but George was able to spend it ten times faster than he received it!

By the middle of the first year, George was desperate for money. He owed money to the tavern owner, the haberdasher, with whom he played cards, and several of his friends. He had to come up with a plan to quickly get more money. Just then, the allowance from his father arrived and gave him a wonderful idea, which he put into immediate action.

George made a big fuss over the money he had just received, making sure that many people in the school knew it had arrived in the mail. Then he sneaked into his dormitory room and hid the money in the false bottom of his trunk. Next, he took a hammer and smashed the lock on the trunk, as well as the one on his guitar case. Then he grabbed his coat and went for a walk. Throughout the walk he practiced what he would say, and by the time he got back to school he had everything rehearsed perfectly.

He strolled in through the front door, commenting on the pleasant weather to some of the other students as he took his coat off. He then walked into his room, looked at the broken lock on his trunk, and yelled. Young men came running to see what had happened.

"My money," George yelled, enjoying himself immensely. "My money's gone. Someone's broken into my trunk and stolen it." He looked at the shocked faces of his friends. "What am I going to do now?" he wailed.

"Don't worry, George, we'll work something out," said one friend.

"Yes, it will be all right," said another friend, patting George kindly on the shoulder.

"I wonder who would do such a thing?" asked a third friend, but any attempt to answer the question was lost in a wave of sympathy.

George smiled to himself. The plan was going better than he'd hoped!

Over the next several days, George's friends took up a collection for him, and when they presented it to him, it added up to more than the amount he had actually "lost." The people he owed money to were also kind and extended the length of their loans. By the time the plan had run its course, George had more than twice as much money as his father had sent him, and he didn't have to pay off his creditors right away. George congratulated himself on outsmarting everyone. And he didn't have the slightest tinge of regret about what he had done. There was nothing to regret; it was all a game.

In the next two years that George spent at school in Nordhausen, no one ever found out what he'd done, or any of the other dishonest things he had done. He had covered his tracks well.

When George's time at Nordhausen was nearly over, Johann Müller sent for George to discuss his future. Mr. Müller announced that he wanted George to become a Lutheran pastor. The Lutheran church was the official state church in Prussia. Lutheran pastors were well paid and well respected. When George learned that his father was prepared to pay for him to attend Halle University to earn his degree, he quickly agreed to enroll. This time there would be no personal tutor!

George Müller couldn't have been happier. He was going to the University of Halle after all. He was also on his way to becoming a Lutheran pastor, a person of high standing in Prussian society. Goodness knows what "tricks" he could play on an entire congregation of kind, gullible people!

Chapter 2

The Life of the Party

George was a little worried. For an hour and a half now he'd been listening to the University of Halle provost's talk about what it meant to be a divinity student, and quite frankly, it sounded rather grim. To be called as pastor to a good, well-paying church, a student had to have both excellent grades, especially in theology, and excellent conduct. "A student who does not show the proper decorum," the provost had droned, his brow knotted into a permanent frown, "will find himself in some tiny, rural church with a meager income and no appropriate social circle."

The mention of the meager income scared George the most. No matter how George and his father fought, Johann Müller had always given his son an ample allowance. Of course, that would end when George graduated and would be responsible for his own financial affairs. That was when he was going to need a good, well-paying church employing him.

George shifted in his seat. His new vest was itching him terribly. With the provost still rambling on, George thought about the outward changes he would need to make for people to believe he was a good candidate to be a Lutheran pastor. First, he would need to purchase a Bible. He had over three hundred books with him, probably more books than any other student at the university, but he did not have a Bible. He would also have to attend church at least every other week. He sighed deeply, but he had no choice. What congregation, after all, would ask a person to be their pastor who went to church no more than three times a year?

Finally, the provost finished his speech, and everyone rose to sing a final hymn. As George emerged from the dingy coolness of the stone chapel into the bright spring sunlight, he told himself that maybe he did need to grow up a little. Partying and playing cards took up a lot of time and money. It was time now for him to stop indulging in such things and throw himself into serious study, especially if he wanted to land in a good church that would pay him a not so meager salary. With this thought in his mind, George wandered off to his room to unpack.

George's good intentions lasted for about two weeks, right up to the time a new friend, Gunter, invited him to Der Grüner Tisch, the wildest ale house in Halle.

"Don't tell me you're too busy to have a little fun," Gunter goaded him.

George put down his book and looked up at Gunter. He hadn't had a drink of beer, heard a good story, or played a round of cards since arriving at the university. He was getting all his studies done, but what was the use of working so hard without a little excitement?

"You're quite right, Gunter," said George, slamming his book shut. "Even a divinity student needs to live a little!" Grabbing his coat, he followed his friend out into the mild April evening.

It wasn't until George was breathing the smoky air, winking at the barmaids, and playing round after round of cards that he realized just how much he had missed it all. This was the life for him. As he gulped his beer, he promised himself that while he partied in the evenings he would keep up his grades during the daytime. Later, when he was closer to graduating, he would worry about being a more suitable candidate for a pastor. After all, he had plenty of time to improve—he was only nineteen years old!

George's reputation soon spread. Everyone at Halle heard about the clever divinity student who could guzzle ten pints of beer in a single sitting, could tell the most outrageous stories, including one about being thrown in jail, and always was ready to gamble. George became so popular that he found himself enjoying Halle more than he'd imagined he would, except for one thing—the old problem of debt. He'd lost a few games of cards and paid for a few rounds of drinks at Der Grüner Tisch and now owed money again. He pawned the watch his father had given him as a confirmation gift five years before, then his towels, sheets, and some of his clothes. He intended to reclaim it all just as soon as he had a big win at cards. The cards did not fall his way, however, and George began borrowing money, just as he had at Nordhausen.

As George strolled along the River Saale one afternoon, feeling a little depressed about being in debt again, he decided he really had to do something about his life. But what? It was so hard trying to change, especially when the ale house was the most exciting place in the entire town. And a young man was entitled to a little excitement. Before he knew it, he was turning the corner and slipping in the door to Der Grüner Tisch.

"Ha, come here, George Müller," he heard Gunter yell over the hubbub in the room. "If there's one thing I know will liven up any party, it's my friend George!"

George grinned, bought himself a pint of beer, and made his way over to the table. Gunter continued the introduction. "This is Herr George Müller, the only divinity student I know who's spent a Christmas in jail. Come on, George, there's some new people here tonight. Tell us all about it."

With great gusto, George launched into his

story. He described the way he had tricked the first innkeeper and the look on the face of the policeman as he had grabbed George. It all seemed so funny now, and George reveled in reliving and embellishing the story with each telling. As he spoke, he glanced around at the listening crowd. Gunter was right—there were some faces he'd never seen before. Through the smoky haze, though, the man sitting at the far end of the table looked vaguely familiar.

"Well told," laughed Gunter, slapping George heartily on the back when he finished the story. "I'll get you another beer, and then I want you to tell the story about when you broke into the pawn shop and retrieved your trunk."

"Yes, yes. Get me a drink, and I'll tell you another story," agreed George, happy to be the center of attention.

As the group around the table laughed among themselves, George noticed the man at the far end get up and walk towards him. *Yes,* he frowned, *I've seen him before, but where*?

"Beta's the name," said the man, thrusting his hand out to shake George's. "I don't suppose you remember me, though I remember you well."

George reached back into his memory. Beta. Beta. Then it came to him. "Ah, Beta, how good to see you! Of course, I remember you from the Cathedral Classical School at Halberstadt. You were the one who always carried the Bible and went to prayer meetings."

Beta turned red. "Yes," he stammered, "but I've decided to live a little now that I'm at Halle. Can we be friends?"

George wasn't sure that was a good idea. On the one hand he felt a strange rush of hope seeing the religious Beta again. For just a second he even thought Beta might be able to help him get out of the mess he was in! On the other hand, the last thing he wanted was to be seen with a religious do-gooder, though from the way Beta sounded, it seemed he might want to put those days behind him. "Let's see what happens," George said noncommittally, at the same time moving over to make room for Gunter.

The night finished like so many others, with George helping a few of his very drunk friends find their way back to their rooms. But as he did so tonight, Beta followed along behind him, chattering away about their time at Halberstadt. *He's very eager to be friends,* thought George as he steadied Gunter, who was staggering along beside him. *I guess there is no harm in his tagging along with us.*

Soon the semester was nearly over, and the summer holidays were just around the corner. George pondered the question of what to do for them. Going back to visit his father seemed like a bad idea, and he'd had enough of Halle for a while. What he needed was some fresh air and a change of scenery. What he needed was a trip to Switzerland!

"Switzerland?" said Beta incredulously. "How can we afford to go to Switzerland?"

George smiled. "You worry too much," he scolded his friend. "Trust me. I have a plan. I always do. Once our exams are over, we won't need our books until next year, will we?"

Beta nodded in agreement.

"Well, instead of letting them lie around in our rooms, let's pawn them and use the money for our trip. When we get back, we can use our first installment of allowance money to get them back. Now doesn't that sound like a plan?"

"Well...," Beta's voice trailed off. "I guess it could work, as long as we knew we could get the books back."

"Of course we will. Trust me," replied George, as if the matter were already settled.

"But what about passports? I'm underage, and so are you. Our fathers will have to sign for us."

"You are too honest for your own good, Beta!" laughed George. "You told me you were leaving all that religious stuff behind. Sometimes you just have to get a little creative."

"How?" Beta asked.

George took a deep breath. "How many pieces of paper do you have with your father's signature on them?" he asked.

"Maybe two or three," replied Beta, looking puzzled.

"And how hard it is to practice until you can write your father's signature just like he does?"

A broad smile lit up Beta's face. Finally he was beginning to understand. "You mean forge my father's signature?" he asked.

George nodded. "You can't tell me you've never thought of doing that before," he goaded.

"Well, I, I...What a good idea," Beta stammered. Then sounding more confident, he added, "I'm sure that won't be hard to do at all."

And it wasn't. On August 28, 1825, five young men set out from Halle for Switzerland. Each of them sported a new Prussian passport in his coat pocket, and each of the other four had handed to George a pouch of gold coins. George had offered to keep track of all their expenses on the trip.

The men had a great time. They traveled by horse-drawn coach through Frankfurt, Stuttgart, and Zurich, right into the heart of Switzerland. They slept out in the open fields, climbed tall mountains, swam in glacial lakes, and entertained the local people in the village ale houses they frequented along the way. After a month, the weather began to cool, and it was time for them to begin the journey back to Halle for the fall semester. As they traveled back through Bavaria and into southern Prussia, everyone congratulated George and Beta on their wonderful idea.

As much fun as everyone else had had, George was sure he'd enjoyed the trip the most. That was because he had paid only half as much as his four companions. Helping yourself every so often along the way to a few coins from the combined purse was one of the advantages of being in charge of the money, George rationalized. Besides, if his friends were too stupid to ask questions about how much things cost, they deserved to be swindled!

When they finally arrived back at Halle, George was the only one with enough money to redeem his books from the pawnshop right away. Yes, he smiled to himself as he walked back to his room with his books, it had been a great trip, and profitable, too! He wondered where they would go next year.

By November, life had settled back into a familiar routine for George Müller. George studied hard during the day and partied and gambled by night.

During the afternoon of November 20, as George studied hard in his room, Beta dropped by to visit. "How about a walk?" he asked. "It's stopped snowing, and the paths have been cleared."

George looked up from his English textbook. A walk did seem like a good idea. It might help clear his head.

Beta waited patiently while George finished reading the page he was on and then pulled on his overcoat. The two of them headed outside and began walking towards the river.

"I wonder if Otto will be at Der Grüner Tisch tonight. He tells a great story about his days in the army, doesn't he?" said George as they walked side by side.

Beta nodded. "Yes, he does, but I won't be going along tonight. I have something else to do."

"Something else?" mocked George. "Something more important than a drink with your friends! And what might that something be?"

Beta looked away. "I've met another old friend," he said.

"Anyone I know?" inquired George.

"It's Herr Kayser. I don't think you know him," Beta replied.

"Well, how do you know this Herr Kayser?"

Beta began fiddling with the fringe of his scarf. "Well, he's...," he began, then stopped. Then he blurted, "I'm going to a Bible meeting, and he's going to be running it."

"A Bible meeting?" laughed George out loud. "Beta, I thought you had left all that behind when you met me!"

"I just wanted to have some fun. I never said I was giving it all up completely," Beta said lamely.

"Well, you have turned religious on me again, have you? What do you do at these meetings?'

"Nothing that you'd be interested in," Beta replied. "We sing and pray, and Herr Kayser reads a sermon. It's not that bad, really. I think you'd even like Herr Kayser if you met him."

A scene flashed through George's mind. George was at Der Grüner Tisch telling his latest and funniest story yet—about the night he'd gone with Beta to a Bible meeting!

"I will meet Herr Kayser," said George, turning to face his friend, "tonight, with you."

Beta's face turned as white as the snow they were trudging through. "No, I don't want you to. I mean, you don't have to," he said stumbling over his words.

"Nonsense, Beta. You always go to the ale house with me. The least I can do is to go to a Bible meeting with you," George said mockingly, enjoying his friend's discomfort.

George and Beta continued the rest of the walk in silence. As the snow crunched under his feet, George wondered what he had agreed to. It was fun to see Beta so worried, but was it worth his time going to a Bible meeting? He had heard about them. Sometimes people even got arrested at them for delivering sermons. It was against the law in Prussia to give a sermon without a registered Lutheran pastor present. This was supposed to ensure that only university-trained pastors got to preach, which kept the Bible from being distorted and uneducated peasants from getting strange ideas. At least that was what George had always been told.

According to Beta, however, Herr Kayser was going to *read* the sermon. That was how people got around the law. As long as the sermon had originally been written by a licensed and trained pastor, it could be read at any gathering. That got George wondering about what kind of man would want to read someone else's sermon. And more important, what was George getting himself into by going to the Bible meeting to hear someone else's sermon being read?

Chapter 3

Something Was Strangely Different

A tall, burly, blond man reached out to take George's coat. "I am Herr Wagner. Welcome to my home," he said.

George mumbled something in reply. He was already beginning to regret coming. Perhaps the fresh supply of stories he had hoped to garner by attending the Bible meeting wasn't such a good idea after all.

"You look chilled to the bone, Herr Müller. I suggest you stand by the fire for a few moments and warm yourself before the meeting starts," continued Herr Wagner kindly.

George followed Beta into a large library where twelve men and women were already seated in a semicircle around the blazing fire. Beta motioned towards a seat near the door, and George was glad to slip into it. He had never felt so out of place in his life.

Soon a hymnbook was thrust into his hand, and George sang along with the others, relieved that at least he recognized the tune of the song. While he sang he relaxed a little and looked around the room. As he glanced to his left, a pair of the prettiest blue eyes he'd ever seen met his. George flushed a little and quickly returned his gaze to the words of the song in the hymnal.

The group sang another hymn and then another. When they finally stopped singing, one of the men—Beta whispered to George that it was Herr Kayser—knelt beside his chair.

"Let us bow our heads in prayer," he began.

George was stunned. He could not take his eyes off Herr Kayser. In his entire life, he had never seen a person kneel to pray. And not only was Herr Kayser kneeling to pray, but he was doing so in a room filled with people. George had always thought that people prayed and sang and taught the Bible the way he'd always heard and seen it done at school and university. But that was not true. Herr Kayser was praying to the same God, but in a totally different way than George had expected. George wondered what else might be different. Before long, he found out.

After a long prayer, Herr Kayser got to his feet, then sat down heavily. He picked up and opened a black leather-bound Bible. He began to read, first a verse, then two, then ten, finally a whole chapter. George looked around. Everyone in the room was concentrating on what was being read. Several people were even nodding in agreement or smiling as certain verses were read. Once the Bible reading was over, Herr Kayser pulled some sheets of paper from the folder on the table beside him, slanted them towards the oil lamp, and began to read the sermon.

George had heard sermons before—at confirmation, at his mother's funeral, and on those few occasions when he'd managed to get up early enough on Sunday to make it to church. But he had never heard a sermon like this one. It wasn't so much the words, but the way they were spoken. Even though Herr Kayser was reading the sermon, he spoke as if every word was important. No—more than important—vital. George felt himself being drawn into what was being read. When Herr Kayser finished reading, George pulled out his watch to check the time. He was surprised to find that an hour and a half had slipped by.

The group sang another hymn, and Herr Wagner announced that it was time for the final prayer. "Dear heavenly Father," he began, "we ask You to forgive us for all our unbelief and to strengthen us to do Your will, trying in all things to honor You and the work of Your beloved son Jesus Christ. Amen."

Once again, George was amazed. It sounded as if Herr Wagner was talking to someone in the room! George sat in his chair for several minutes after the amen, thinking about it. He was stunned by the whole evening. It was not at all like he'd imagined it would be. Beta had told him that Herr Wagner had never been to university. "Yet for all of that," George mumbled to himself, "he prays a better prayer than me, and I'm a divinity student."

"What did you say?" asked Beta, his voice breaking into George's thoughts.

"Nothing," said George.

But it was something. These people sang as if they were singing about someone they knew. They prayed as if they were praying to someone in the room. And they preached as if they believed every word they said. It was all very troubling to George.

"Are you ready to go? Or should we ask if we can spend the night?" joked Beta.

George looked around, startled to notice that only a couple of people were still in the room. One of them was the young woman who had been staring at him during the singing of the first hymn. Now she walked boldly over to him. "Aren't you going to introduce me to your friend, Beta?" she asked in a lilting voice.

"Yes, of course," replied Beta. "Ermegarde, I would like you to meet a college friend of mine, George Müller."

George bowed, and Ermegarde nodded, causing her ringlets to bounce around the edges of her face. "I hope we shall be seeing more of you, Herr Müller," she said, looking coyly into his eyes.

"Yes, yes," said George, desperately looking for a way out. He was not used to talking to women, unless he was at the ale house half drunk!

"We must be off, George," said Beta, rescuing him.

George put on his coat, scarf, and gloves and followed Beta out into the cold, snowy night. The two men silently trotted alongside each other as they made their way back to the university.

Finally, Beta broke the silence. "Well, what did you think of the meeting?"

George could have come up with a funny reply, but for once he felt serious. He answered truthfully. "Nothing I have ever done, not traveling to Switzerland, not spending the night drinking and partying at Der Grüner Tisch, has ever been as enjoyable to me as this evening."

"Then you must come back with me tomorrow afternoon. They are having another meeting," said Beta with a look of amazement in his eyes.

George did go back the next day, and the day after that, too. Before the week was over, George Müller was kneeling beside his bed asking God to forgive him his sins so that he could become a true Christian.

All of this was an abrupt about-face for George. Many of his friends from Der Grüner Tisch found it impossible to believe it was not some elaborate trick. But as the days went by, even they had to admit that something was strangely different about George. He certainly wasn't the old George Müller they had spent so many nights at the ale house with. This George didn't want to drink beer with them anymore. He didn't want to go to parties. He didn't want to borrow money. He didn't even want to tell funny stories about his narrow escapes. All he seemed to want to do now was read the new Bible he had bought for himself and ask people questions about God and what they thought of religion. And he was always going off to those strange meetings where people read sermons when it wasn't even Sunday!

George's friends were revolted by the change. George was acting worse than any divinity student they knew, and they made sure to tell him so. But their remarks had no effect. George had found the most exciting thing in the world, and he wasn't going to give it up for anyone. Of course, meeting Ermegarde at each meeting he attended was an added bonus. George came to look forward to her flattering talk and dazzling smile.

It took George only six weeks of going to the meetings and reading his Bible to come to a remarkable conclusion—one that would define the rest of his life. He concluded that he should be a missionary. It was all very clear to him. There were people in the world who had never heard of God, Jesus Christ, or the gospel message, and George Müller was going to search them out and tell them the good news. Once he'd made his decision, he couldn't wait to tell Ermegarde. Since Ermegarde had attended the same meetings he had, he reasoned that she surely would share the same goal.

The couple found a few moments together after the meeting on the following Saturday. Ermegarde patted the seat beside her at the harpsichord. "Come and sit with me, George. I want to hear you play a hymn," she said coyly.

"I don't want to play right now, Ermegarde," he replied. "I have something to talk to you about."

George sat down beside her and held her hand. "Ermegarde, I have decided to become a missionary," he said, relieved to finally have his plan out in the open.

Ermegarde gasped. "Why George, whatever made you think of such a ridiculous thing? I could never be a missionary's wife!" Her face turned bright red as she realized what she'd said. George had not officially asked her yet.

There was a long moment of silence. George was the first to break it. "Well, I think you would make a very good missionary's wife. We could learn together, don't you think?" he asked hopefully.

Ermegarde turned up her nose. "You can't be serious. I could never be a missionary. Missionaries are poor; they wear drab clothes and ride in carriages I wouldn't be seen dead in. I'm sorry, George Müller, but it's the mission field or me. I would gladly be your wife, but I would never be the wife of a missionary. You have a good mind. Be a lawyer or a doctor, and leave being a missionary for other people who don't have anything better to do!" With that she stood up and stomped out of the room.

George went home that night feeling very dejected. He liked Ermegarde. He might even love her. He wasn't sure. She was pretty and funny and, up until tonight, he'd thought, spiritually minded. But now she had left him with a choice, a choice he agonized over for several weeks. In the end, George told Ermegarde he was going to continue his quest to become a missionary, and if she did not want to marry a missionary, obviously she did not want to marry him.

Although it was a difficult decision to come to, George felt much better once he'd announced it. He began to read every paper and report he could find about missionaries. Soon, much to his delight, he was invited to hear a real missionary speak. The man was Herman Ball, and he came from a wealthy family. Instead of living the kind of rich, lazy life he could easily have afforded, Herman Ball chose to work in Poland among the Jews in the ghettos of Warsaw.

When George heard Herman Ball speak, he was inspired. He knew exactly what he should do! He should transfer from Halle University to the missionary training school Herr Wagner had told him about. Then he should go off and be a missionary, just like Herman Ball. But first he needed to tell someone about his new life and career change: his father.

It was now summertime, and the Prussian countryside was in full bloom. As George Müller looked out the coach window, he hardly noticed. He had other things on his mind. He fingered the papers tucked in his coat pocket. He tried to imagine what his father would say when he was asked to sign the papers that would transfer his son to the missionary training school. Surely, he reasoned, his father would not be too upset. After all, George had given up stealing, cheating, and lying. That was something. At least George thought it was. Even the fact he was asking his father to sign the papers instead of forging his signature, as he usually did, was a sign of a big change in George. Despite this reasoning, George had a gnawing feeling that every crack of the coachman's whip was taking him closer to a confrontation with his father.

"You want me to what?" Johann Müller bellowed, his eyes bulging in frenzied anger. "Have you gone mad? What is wrong with you, boy?"

George explained there was nothing wrong with him anymore. In fact, he felt things were more right with him than they had ever been in his entire life. He had stopped drinking, gambling, and partying, all things his father had nagged him for years to give up, and in their place he went to church three times a week, read his Bible each day, and prayed regularly. On top of all this, in the past six months he'd pulled his grades up to the highest level. "You always wanted me to be a Lutheran pastor. Now I want to be a missionary. That isn't so different. Both are callings that honor God," George added at the end.

"Honor! Don't talk to me about honor."

George could hear his father's voice rising to a dangerous pitch. For a moment he wondered whether he would be beaten as he'd been so often as a child. But he was twenty-one years old now. Surely his father would not beat him.

"What is the fifth commandment? Tell me that." demanded his father.

George sighed. "Honor your father and mother," he said, sensing where his father was headed with this line of questioning.

Sure enough, Johann Müller thrust his face close to his son's and asked, "And did you honor your dear mother? Did you? What about the day she died? When I went to fetch you at Halberstadt they told me you were at a party, drinking and playing cards. You didn't come back until 2 A.M., and your mother was dead by then. How is that honoring your mother?"

George could feel his father's hot breath against his cheeks. He did not answer, and Johann Müller let the question hang in the air for a moment before pressing on. "And now, you think you are honoring me with this wild scheme? What will my friends say? 'Poor Johann Müller, he paid for his son to go to school until he was twenty-one. Halle University, no less! A bright lad, too, top of the class. Yes, he was going to be a Lutheran pastor, a good position with a good salary and respect, and then he threw it all away and became a missionary with not even a penny in his pocket.'" Mr. Müller viciously spat out the word missionary. "Do you think I invested all this money in your education so you could do this to me? God help me, George, I'll disown you if you do this to me."

Then his father did something George would never have predicted. He burst into tears. "Don't do this, George, I beg of you. Don't do this." He sobbed deeply as he clung to his son's coat sleeve.

George sat on the edge of his chair. He did not know which was worse, his father ranting or his father sobbing.

After a minute or so, his father pointed to the library door. "Go," he gasped between sobs. "Get out of my sight."

George quietly got up and left the room. The confrontation he'd feared had occurred.

Over the next two days, George did everything possible to change his father's mind. He knew that unless his father signed the papers he could not transfer into the missionary training school. Despite his son's best efforts, George's father was unmoved. He made his position perfectly clear to his son. He had spent a lot of money on George's education, and he expected results. Most notably, he wanted to eventually see his son in a good, well-paying position in a Lutheran church. George could not guarantee such a result. He had promised to do whatever God asked of him and so could not be bound by his father's wishes. So, on the morning before he was due to go back to Halle University, George knocked on the library door.

"Come in," his father said. When he saw it was George, he added impatiently, "Well, what is it?"

George took a deep breath. "I have come to a decision," he said, holding his hands behind his back so his father would not see they were shaking.

"So you've come to your senses at last?" Johann Müller growled.

"Actually, Father, I feel very clear-headed. I have decided that it would not be right for me to take any more money from you, since I cannot guarantee I will do what you want or that I can pay you back in kind or in a good reputation." George could see his father's face turning bright red, but he could not stop quite yet. "Since you will not sign the papers for me to go to the missionary training school, I will remain at Halle until I get my degree. But in so doing, I will not take one more penny of your money, not for tuition, not for books, not for food. Not one penny," and then he added boldly, "ever!"

Johann Müller looked at his oldest son with narrow, blazing eyes. "So be it," he hissed. "Now get out of my sight."

George turned and left the room. As he shut the door behind him, he knew he'd also closed a door in his life. Whatever his faults, his father had always given him an allowance, bailed him out of jail, and sent extra money when he needed more books. Now he, George Müller, student at the University of Halle and soon-to-be missionary, had shut the door on his father's money, now and forever.

Later that day, as George sat in the stagecoach rumbling back towards Halle, he felt strangely relieved. The sense of looming confrontation he'd felt on the journey home had been replaced with a sense of expectation. He had been given no choice but to cut the ties with his earthly father. Now all he had was his heavenly Father to provide for him. As the villages and fields slipped by, George wondered how it would all work out.

Chapter 4

Too Childish for a Grown Man

George Müller drummed his fingers on his desk. "Money," he mumbled to himself, barely audibly, "I need money." A year ago he wouldn't have been sitting in his room worrying about the money he needed. He would have been out doing something about it. There had always been a way to get what he needed. There was someone he could borrow from, something he could pawn. He could even getting lucky playing a few rounds of cards. But not now. Now George was a Christian and would not use any of his old tricks or schemes to raise the money he needed. There had to be some other way, but what was it? He'd tried to find work at several businesses, but all the jobs had been promised to students long before they left for summer vacation.

As he gazed out the window at the trees now laden with golden leaves, George had a strange idea. At first he resisted it. It was too childish for a grown man and much too simple for a university student. It would be foolish to kneel down and ask God to send him the money he needed. He had never heard of anyone doing that! God wasn't interested in what George Müller ate for dinner or whether he had textbooks to study from. Or was He? Finally, George decided to try it anyway. He slipped to his knees and leaned his elbows on the edge of his bed. "Dear God," he began, wondering whether he was making a fool of himself. "You know the situation I'm in, and You know what I need. I ask You to provide for me. Amen."

There, he had done it. He stood up and ran his hands through his thick, brown hair. Now he would wait and see what happened.

An hour later as George was rewriting some lecture notes, he was interrupted by a firm knock at the door. "Come in," he yelled, assuming it to be one of his friends.

The door swung open, and standing in the doorway was none other than Dr. Tholuck, Halle University's new professor of divinity, and with him a stranger. George jumped to his feet in astonishment, wondering what on earth the professor was doing at his doorway. He bowed politely, spilling papers everywhere as he did so. "I am sorry, sir," he said, unsure of what to do next. "Would you like to come in?"

George glanced quickly around his room. His books were sprawled out on his bed, and a half-drunk cup of coffee and a trail of crumbs lay on his desk. The two men entered the room.

"Thank you," said Dr. Tholuck, who then turned to the stranger and began to speak to him in English. George soon realized why the professor was speaking English. "Dr. Hodge, this is George Müller, the man I told you so much about. George, this is Dr. Hodge from Princeton University in America."

Dr. Hodge smiled warmly but said nothing.

George bowed again. He could not think of anything else to do or why on earth these two distinguished men were crammed into his tiny room.

"I will get right to the point," Dr. Tholuck went on, clearing his throat. "Dr. Hodge and three of his colleagues from America have come to visit Halle for a year. They will be attending lectures and, as time goes by, giving them as well. There is just one difficulty. None of them speaks German."

"Oh," said George, wondering how any of this involved him.

Dr. Tholuck smiled. "I have been told you speak English well and that you would make an excellent tutor for our guests."

George could feel himself getting a little flustered. This was the last thing he needed. If he volunteered to help four people learn English, he would have no time at all to earn money even if he did find a job. He had to think of a polite way to say no.

"I am honored," he stammered, reverting back to German in the hope of not embarrassing Dr. Hodge. "It's just that it would be hard to find the time. My circumstances have changed a little this year, and I have been forced to look for a job." He smiled, hoping Dr. Tholuck would not be insulted.

"Why George," laughed Dr. Tholuck. "You don't think I would ask you to do this for nothing, do you? This *is* a job!"

"I see," said George with a lot more excitement in his voice.

"You must discuss the rate with Dr. Hodge. Take the job only if it pays enough," advised Dr. Tholuck.

Feeling a little awkward about the situation, George turned to the American. He spoke in English again. "I hear you would like me to tutor you in German," he said.

"Yes," replied Dr. Hodge with a strong American accent. "And if you do it half as well as the professor promises me you will, we'll be glad to pay you twice the going rate. Now let's work out the details, shall we?"

Fifteen minutes later, it was all settled. George would tutor the four Americans for eight hours a week. Even though they would come to lessons together, Dr. Hodge insisted they would each be happy to pay him separately, and double the normal rate. George's eyes widened as he added it up. This meant he would be getting eight times as much as a regular tutor would be paid. He tried to protest that it was too much, but Dr. Hodge just smiled and told him not to worry about it. The money had already been set aside.

As George opened the door to bid his guests farewell, Dr. Tholuck turned to him and said, "Maybe there is something else you might be interested in, George. Apparently there's an orphanage across the street, the Franke Orphanage, I believe it's called. Anyway, they have a room set aside for a divinity student. It's nothing fancy from what I understand, but deserving students are selected to stay there free for two months at a time. Have you heard of it?"

George nodded. "Yes, I have, sir," he replied, recollecting the way he and his friends at the ale house had made fun of the poor, unfortunate students who'd been forced to stay there. But now, for some reason, it sounded like somewhere he would like to stay.

"I have to submit a list of names of worthy students. Would you like me to put your name on the list?" asked Dr. Tholuck, looking directly into George's deep blue eyes.

"Yes, sir. Thank you. I would be very grateful if you would."

"I thought you might. From what I've heard, it seems like the kind of thing you'd be interested in. Well, I must get Dr. Hodge back to his room so he can finish unpacking. Good day to you, George."

"Nice to meet you, son," said the American, flashing him a smile.

With that, the two men were gone.

George walked back to his desk and sat down. He felt like he was in a dream. He pulled his watch from his pocket. It had been only an hour and a half since he'd prayed. And now he had a well-paying job and the possibility of a free room for two months. He knelt at his bedside for the second time that afternoon and gave thanks to God.

As it turned out, George Müller was the second student to get to use the room at the orphanage that year. He moved his few belongings up the five flights of stairs to the room on the top floor with the dull view of the gray stone building directly across the street.

While the view from the room might have been dull, life at the orphanage was certainly lively! George had walked past the orphanage nearly every day since arriving in Halle, but he had no idea how or why it had been founded. When he heard the story, he was fascinated by it. Dr. A. H. Franke had been a professor of theology at Halle University a hundred years before. Since Dr. Franke was a dedicated Christian, he felt God had called him to help the orphans in the town. With no rich family connections and only a little money of his own, he had managed to scrape together enough to build the large six-story building. From there he had fed, clothed, housed, and educated two thousand children. Even now, George was told, the orphanage had no regular source of income, and those who ran it relied upon God to supply their needs. Because Dr. Franke had been a professor at

Halle, he had stated in his will that one room of the orphanage was to be permanently set aside for deserving students to use free of charge.

George was in awe of Dr. Franke's story, which made his prayer asking for enough money to make it through the year seem puny by comparison. He wondered how a person ever got to have faith like Dr. Franke's.

While George was staying at the orphanage, he was invited to give his first sermon at a small countryside church. This was an important moment for a divinity student, and George fretted about what he should say. He skimmed through many books looking for something that sounded grand enough. Once he had selected a passage, he wrote out his sermon, correcting and recorrecting it, trying first one word and then another. Satisfied that he could improve it no more, he submitted it to a professor for approval. Once it was approved, he committed the entire half-hour sermon to memory. He did not want to read it from the page when he delivered it, and he did not want to get caught for a single second without knowing what he was going to say next.

Finally, Sunday, August 27, 1826, arrived. George borrowed a horse and rode out into the countryside to the dot on the map where he was assured there was a church. Sure enough, as he approached the location, there it was, nestled among the trees, its bell chiming that it was time for the service to begin. George hurried in and met the elderly pastor. Then he quickly checked out the pulpit to reassure himself that everything was in order.

George stood nervously picking at one of his coat buttons as the last strains of the hymn faded. He adjusted the collar of his shirt and stood to speak. He began exactly as he had planned. With growing satisfaction he realized he could recite the sermon perfectly. He put emphasis on the right words and paused just long enough for the right dramatic effect. His voice rose and fell evenly, and by the end of the sermon he was congratulating himself. It was a near perfect performance.

As George stood at the door after the service, shaking hands with members of the congregation, his attitude quickly changed. The congregation consisted of poor, rural people, mostly farmers. Several of them thanked George for his "very fancy sermon." Others laughed and said they hadn't understood a word he'd said.

George ate lunch with the elderly pastor of the church. He tried to be polite, but his mind was not really on the conversation. Instead, he was thinking about his sermon, the very sermon a week before he had thought was a brilliantly polished masterpiece. But what had seemed polished and alive to him had been dead and irrelevant to his hearers. George could rationalize that they were just illiterate farmers and unable to grasp the simplest of concepts taught in university, but he was starting to see things from a different perspective. The purpose of a sermon was not for the preacher to show how many long words he could string together or how many important books he could mention. No, the purpose of a sermon was to instruct people about how to know God, and for that purpose, the simpler it was, the better.

By the end of lunch, George had made a decision. He was not ever again going to preach as he had that morning. Rather, he was going to preach using simple words and ideas, and he would quote only from the Bible.

Later that afternoon he had a chance to try out his new approach to delivering sermons. He was scheduled to speak at the afternoon service in the church. Originally, he had intended to deliver the same sermon again, but not now. He folded the pages the sermon was written on and put them back in his pouch. Instead, he pulled out his Bible. "Is there somewhere I could be alone for a few minutes to pray?" he politely asked.

The old pastor seemed surprised by the request. "Well, yes, you can stay here if you like. I always take a stroll in the garden after lunch. I was going to ask you to join me, but if you would rather stay here and pray…." His voice trailed off.

"Thank you," George replied. "I think I need to."

When the old pastor had gone, George sank to his knees beside his chair. "Dear God," he prayed simply, "show me what you want me to say this afternoon." With that he opened his Bible to the Book of Matthew, chapter five, to the passage he had been reading that morning back at Halle.

Before long some ideas came to him based around the verse "Blessed are the poor in spirit."

George thanked God for His help and stood up. There would be no fancy, high-sounding sermon this afternoon, just a few simple thoughts from the New Testament.

That afternoon, the congregation left the church with smiles on their faces. "I think I learned something this afternoon," said one farmer with calloused hands.

"You really made things come alive," said an old woman, her brown eyes shining.

George rode back to Halle a happy man. He had learned a lesson, a lesson he vowed never to forget.

The rest of the year passed quickly for George. He was asked to give more sermons, and he made sure they were always simple messages from his heart. He went to the Bible meeting every Saturday, and on Sunday mornings he would walk ten or fifteen miles to hear a good preacher. On Sunday evenings, a group of Christian men from Halle met in his room for prayer and hymn singing.

Exactly a year after George had delivered his first sermon, a letter addressed to Dr. Tholuck arrived at Halle University from the Continental Missionary Society in England. The letter asked Dr. Tholuck if he had a student he could recommend to be a missionary in the city of Bucharest in southeastern Europe. Dr. Tholuck wasted no time in asking George if he was interested. After praying about it, George agreed to fill out the application papers and send them back to London. He felt sure he would get the position because, much to his surprise, his father had agreed to let him go. He saw this as a sign of God's blessing on the endeavor.

As George waited for a reply from London, he kept busy with his studies, which included English, Greek, German, French, Latin, and Italian. Along with studying these languages, George felt a need to study Hebrew. He couldn't think of a good reason why he felt this way, since he did not know a single Jewish person. Yet, he bought a Hebrew textbook from which he taught himself the language as best he could.

About a month after sending the application papers off to London, George happened to be meeting with Dr. Tholuck. As they talked, the professor asked out of the blue, "Have you ever thought of being a missionary to the Jews? I'm an adviser to the London Society for Promoting Christianity Among the Jews. Did you know that?"

"No, sir, I did not," replied George, thinking the question odd, since Dr. Tholuck already knew he intended to go to Bucharest. "But it is strange you should ask. I have had a peculiar desire to study Hebrew for the last while."

"Well, perhaps you should consider it," urged the professor. "I know you want to go to Bucharest, so I suggest you pray and wait. If things work out for you to go to Bucharest, you should take that as God's will and go. But if not, perhaps His will is for you to work with the Jews."

George nodded. He would keep learning Hebrew and wait. As it turned out, he didn't have to wait long. Later that month he received a letter from the Continental Missionary Society thanking him for his interest in Bucharest. They were sorry to inform him, however, that they were no longer able to send a missionary there. A war between Russia and Turkey was going on in the area that made it unsafe for missionary work to proceed. They would, however, keep his application on file in case the situation changed, although they did not think that was likely in the next year or two.

As George read the letter, a sense of relief swept over him. God had made His will plain. George was not supposed to go to Bucharest as a missionary after all. George asked Dr. Tholuck if he would submit his name to the London Society for Promoting Christianity Among the Jews as a missionary candidate. Dr. Tholuck happily obliged, sending off a letter immediately. Then both men waited, and waited, and waited some more for a reply. In May 1828, while he was still waiting for a reply, George completed his degree and found a temporary job as a chaplain.

Finally in June, George Müller received his reply. The London Society for Promoting Christianity Among the Jews had reviewed Dr. Tholuck's letter and was prepared to offer George a six-month probationary period in London, to start at his convenience. George would spend his time studying the Hebrew language and effective ways to communicate with

Jews. At first George was upset. He had waited so long for a reply, and now he was being told he needed to travel all the way to London for six more months of study. He had been studying all his life, it seemed. In the end, he took up the offer. After all, it appeared it was God's will for him to do so.

In his eagerness to get to London, however, George had overlooked one very important matter. Prussia had an army that was the envy of every other country in Europe. The army had become renowned through its practice of conscription. Prussia was the first nation in modern Europe to require all her able-bodied men to serve in the army. Conscripts served three years in the army, although men with a university degree were required to serve only one year. There was no way George would be allowed to leave Prussia until he had served his one year in the army. The trouble was, he didn't have a year to spare. He wanted to get to London as soon as possible. So, he began to pray....

Chapter 5

A Free Man

George lay in bed, his head throbbing with pain and his eyes feeling like two burning cinders. He was vaguely aware of a doctor standing over him, pushing and prodding on his abdomen. He winced in pain with each touch. It felt as though the doctor was stabbing him with a knife. George heard the doctor talking to someone else in the room. Was it Beta? He tried to pull all his mental faculties together and concentrate, but he couldn't. He sank back onto his pillow as the darkness of unconsciousness overcame him.

Several hours later he awoke. His sheets were drenched with perspiration, and his head still throbbed. He didn't think anyone else was in the room, and he lay quietly wondering whether this was it.

"So this is how it's going to end. It's no wonder I didn't get an exemption from the army so I could go to England. I wasn't supposed to go anywhere. I'm going to die in Prussia." George mumbled to himself, the words barely audible above his shallow breathing. The thought of dying did not scare George. In fact, George felt strangely peaceful and resigned to his fate. It was true he had done all he could to get out of his army obligations. He had written to explain that he wanted to be a missionary. That had not worked. He'd had important officials appeal directly to King Frederick William III on his behalf. The king had refused the appeals. In the end, there had been no alternative. George was to report for army duty in a month. But now he would be going nowhere.

George heard door hinges creak and looked over to see Beta silhouetted in the doorway. Beta tiptoed to the bedside. When he saw that George was awake, he smiled. "How are you feeling, my friend?" he asked quietly.

"I don't know. Better, I think," replied George, unsure of his condition. "Did the doctor come to see me before?"

"Yes," replied Beta, surprised. "You remember?"

George tried to nod his head, but it hurt too much. "What did he say?" he asked.

"It's not good news, I'm afraid. It seems the illness you have had for the past month made you cough and overexercise your stomach muscles. The coughing fit caused a blood vessel in your stomach to break. You had been bleeding there for quite some time, the doctor thought."

"What happens now?" asked George through cracked lips.

"I have some medicine here the doctor mixed for you. He said you should take it and rest and pray."

Beta lifted an amber-colored bottle from the sidetable and pulled the cork from its neck. George swallowed a spoonful of the thick, black liquid from the bottle before falling back onto his pillow. He was exhausted from the effort of leaning forward.

Rest and pray. George knew how to do both, but would they be enough? For five days George lay somewhere between life and death. Then, much to the amazement of the doctor, he began to make a slow recovery.

A month later, George was well enough to report to the army to begin active duty, or so he thought. As the army doctor examined him—not once but twice—he frowned and asked George a lot of questions about his health. In the end, he shook his head.

"It's a sorry thing to have to say to a young lad like you, but it's my opinion you're not well enough to serve in the army. If you waited ten years, I doubt you'd ever be well enough for the Prussian army. You'll have to be excused."

The doctor looked apologetically at George, who was trying his best to hold back a smile. An army general no less signed the papers, and within the space of an hour, George Müller's sickness had made him a free man, able to travel wherever he wanted!

On March 19, 1829, George stood on the deck of the boat he had boarded in Rotterdam, Holland, for the trip to England. Now as the boat sailed up the River Thames towards London, George took a deep breath of English air. He had made it!

George was eager for the boat to tie up so that he could get on with his training. The sooner he started, the sooner he would be on his way back to mainland Europe as a missionary to the Jews. By the end of his first day in London, George had found himself a room in a cheap boarding house in Hackney, definitely not the fashionable end of London, but it suited his purposes.

The next morning George took a coach to the London Society for Promoting Christianity Among the Jews. There he met the director, who explained to him that every detail of his life for the next six months had been mapped out for him. For twelve hours a day George was to study Hebrew, Chaldee, and the Rabbinic alphabet. At the end of six months, he would be expected to be able to read, write, and speak Hebrew fluently and to recite from memory many chapters from the Old Testament in their original language. When he had proved himself capable of doing this, the society would give him his first missionary assignment, most likely to somewhere in Austria or Russia.

George set to work that evening. Even though he had the advantage of already knowing a little

Hebrew, he was aware that he would have to work hard if he was going to be a missionary at the end of six months.

George encountered small encouragements along the way. He heard, for instance, of a rich dentist from Exeter in southwest England who had given up his very profitable practice to go to Persia as a missionary. The dentist, whose name was Anthony Groves, apparently wasn't asking anyone for financial support. He was going to go out as a missionary, trusting God to meet all of his financial needs. He sounded like a man after George's own heart, and George wished he could have met him. But Dr. Groves had already left England, and all George could do was hope that it wouldn't be too long before he followed Groves's example.

George was in London for only two months before he suffered a setback. The illness that had kept him out of the Prussian army flared up again. The English doctor who visited him was very alarmed. He felt sure that George was about to die, and he urged him to get out of the damp, smoky air of London as soon as possible. He told him that his only hope for recovery was to stay at the seaside.

George took the doctor's advice, and as soon as he had the strength, he made the coach trip to Teignmouth in Devon in southern England. George had no particular reason for choosing Teignmouth other than that it had a mild climate and bracing sea air. But while he was there, he encountered circumstances that would change the course of his life.

While in Teignmouth, George Müller met a Scotsman named Henry Craik. Henry was the same age as George and, like George, was a university graduate who had become a Christian during his college years. Also like George, Henry Craik had worked as a tutor, only not for adults but for children. George was astonished to learn that the children whom Henry had tutored were the children of Anthony Groves, the dentist and now missionary George had heard about in London.

Of course, George wanted to know all about Anthony Groves, and Henry Craik, who was very impressed with his old employer, was glad to share what he knew. He told George that Anthony Groves had become involved with a group of influential Christian men whom he'd encountered while studying in Dublin, Ireland. The men, who were all graduates of top colleges, included in their ranks the sons of an Irish member of Parliament, a baron, a lord, and the godson of Admiral Nelson.

The men had begun meeting together to discuss their Christian beliefs. After studying the Bible, they came to the conclusion that it was indeed true and that they should follow it exactly. This led Anthony Groves to give ten percent of his income to the poor. He then upped it to a quarter. Finally, he began to give away all his income, except for a small amount to cover the day-to-day needs of his family. Ultimately, Groves decided to sell all he had and become a missionary.

Other members of the group made similar decisions. One of them, Benjamin Newton, had begun to hold Christian meetings at Plymouth near the southwestern tip of England, where he was enjoying great success. The meetings were open to believers of all denominations and were now being called the Plymouth Brethren meetings.

George was fascinated by all he heard. He wished he could meet some of these men. If they'd had the kind of impact on Anthony Groves's life as Henry Craik seemed to indicate, they were people George wanted to know.

For ten days George stayed in Teignmouth. He would not allow himself to stay longer, because he had to make up for lost time in his Hebrew lessons. As his health improved and his strength returned, he was more anxious than ever to get on with the task of becoming a missionary.

Although George returned to London feeling physically stronger than he had felt in a long time, something else about him had changed. George had a new mission. He had been inspired by Henry Craik's description of Anthony Groves and the Plymouth Brethren. George promised himself that he would stop reading books *about* the Bible and instead read only the Bible itself from cover to cover. And when he had read through the Bible completely, he would start at the beginning and read it again.

The more George read the Bible, the more he wanted to start doing something right away. He didn't want to wait until he was sent out by the missionary society. George organized a prayer meeting in his room each evening from six until eight. He invited his fellow students, many of whom came to the meetings. But this wasn't enough for George. Why, he asked himself, should he wait until he got to Europe to preach to the Jews? There were thousands of Jews right here in London.

George took to the streets of London, his pockets stuffed with tracts, each with his name and address carefully written on it. He headed for the street corners where he had seen Jewish men gather. Sometimes he preached to the men assembled there, sometimes he read from the New Testament to the small boys who crowded around him, and sometimes he handed out tracts inviting people to visit him.

As he did this, George began to notice something, not something unusual, but something so obvious he'd missed it all along! As he spoke to the Jews, hundreds of non-Jewish people hurried by him. But many of these people needed to hear the gospel message as much as Jewish people did. A desire to talk to people of all religions and faiths about God began to grow in George. It was a desire that would not go away. George began to wonder whether it was right for him to continue his involvement with the London Society for Promoting Christianity Among the Jews. He no longer wanted to go to Europe and work only among the Jews. He wanted to stay in England and preach to anyone who would listen.

On New Year's Day, 1830, he made up his mind. He wrote a letter to the members of the missionary society thanking them for their help and support but asking to be released from their program because he no longer felt sure that God wanted him to return to Europe to preach only to the Jewish people.

On January 27, the board of the society met to consider George Müller's request. Disappointed, they finally agreed to release from their program one of the best students they'd ever had. George was now a free man, a foreigner with nowhere to go, no missionary society to back him, no job, and only a five-pound note in his pocket. He could not have been happier.

Chapter 6

A New Beginning

George Müller looked down from the pulpit at the crowd of bobbing bonnets and balding heads in Ebenezer Chapel at Teignmouth. A lot had happened in the three months since he had left London. George had gone back to Devon to visit his friend Henry Craik, who had arranged for him to preach at a number of various chapels around the area during his visit. Now, twelve weeks later, Ebenezer Chapel had asked him to become its pastor.

As he looked out over the congregation, George knew it had not been an easy decision for the congregation to make. Indeed, a few people had left the church over the young Prussian upstart who thought he could preach to good English Christians! Still, others had been impressed by George's preaching, particularly its results. Five new converts had joined the church as a result of George's preaching and more than filled the spaces made by those who had left the church over George's becoming the new pastor.

When he had finished the morning's sermon, George cleared his throat. "There is one more thing I need to say," he began nervously. "I accept your generous offer to call me as your pastor on one condition. I cannot promise you how long I will stay here. I must be free to go where God leads me, when He leads me. If you will allow me to do that, I will stay and be your pastor."

As George looked down at the small congregation of only eighteen members, he wondered whether he was making a mistake. He had prayed long and hard about taking the position. It seemed strange to him that God would lead him away from a bustling city like London to Teignmouth, a small salmon fishing village on the edge of the Teign estuary where his congregation was made up of mostly unschooled fishermen and their wives.

Still, George reminded himself that if he was prepared to travel, there was plenty of work for a missionary to do in Devon. Christian groups from Newton Abbot to Exeter were eager to have George preach at their weekly Bible studies and prayer meetings. And George was more than happy to do so. Indeed, after officially becoming the pastor at Ebenezer Chapel, George came to know the roads that crisscrossed Devon like he knew the back of his hand.

One place he particularly liked to visit in the summer of 1830 was Northernhay House in Exeter. Northernhay House was a boarding establishment whose housekeeper was a Miss Mary Groves. Mary was a strong Christian in her early thirties who liked to talk with George about religious things, especially his views about the Plymouth Brethren. George had enjoyed several long conversations with her before he realized she was in fact the sister of Anthony Groves, the missionary to Persia he'd heard so much about! It was then that he understood why Mary had so many interesting opinions about missionaries and the church.

The more time he spent with Mary Groves, the more George came to like her. Mary was not a giggly kind of woman like Ermegarde had been. Nor was she pretty like Ermegarde. In fact, she had one of the largest noses George had ever seen on a man or a woman. Yet there was something about her that appealed to him. Mary looked right into his eyes when she spoke, and she expected him to treat her as an equal, not as a decoration. Mary was better educated than most women of her day: She spoke French, Latin, and Hebrew and knew more about astronomy than George did.

The relationship blossomed, and George found himself in love with Mary. Such a feeling surprised him for more than one reason. First, Mary Groves was thirty-three years old, eight years older than he was. And second, he had not been looking for or even considering a wife. As far as he was concerned, a wife would slow him down. What if God called him to go someplace strange or remote? Could he expect a wife to follow him? And would he feel as though marriage had made him a prisoner?

Although George may not have expected just any wife to follow him, there was something different about Mary. Since Mary had seen her brother and sister-in-law give up everything they owned to go to the mission field, George sensed she would be willing to do the same if necessary. He talked to Mary about his fears, and Mary assured him that a godly marriage would set him free to do even more than he was doing now, not the reverse.

On October 7, 1830, in a simple ceremony at Exeter, Mary Groves and George Müller were married. After a cup of tea with friends, they caught the stagecoach to Teignmouth.

As he loaded Mary's trunks onto the stagecoach, George was a little surprised. Two of the four trunks were particularly heavy. "I didn't know you had so much stuff," he muttered.

"You don't think my family was penniless do you?" replied Mary, adjusting the ribbon on her bonnet. "I have the family silver, my mother's china, and several tapestries that have been in the family for generations. I think they will brighten up your house considerably."

A week later all of Mary's possessions were neatly arranged in George's tiny row house, which no longer looked like a bachelor lived in it. Mary had scrubbed and dusted and polished until everything looked well cared for.

One night George came home weary from traveling. Mary met him at the door with a smile. "Come and see how good it all looks," she said, helping her new husband out of his coat. "I have hardly stopped cleaning and arranging all day."

As George looked around the room, his heart sank. His house was beginning to look like so many other houses he had visited—cluttered with things: things that would stop him from answering God's call on his life, things that would have to be packed up and transported from one place to another, things that would mock his attempt to live only for God.

He sank wearily into his chair. "They have to go," he said in a low voice.

"What has to go?" frowned Mary.

"Everything," replied George, waving his hand vaguely around the room, "The silver, the china, the tapestries. Everything that's not necessary has to go."

"But why?" stammered Mary, turning pale and sinking into a chair.

"Because," said George, "I travel from one end of Devon to the other preaching that the Bible is to be taken literally, and I come home at night to a home filled with baubles. After all, Jesus said, 'Sell all you have and give to the poor,' didn't He?"

"Yes, but...," said Mary.

"But what? Your own brother did that, didn't he?" said George, cutting her off.

"But he was going to be a missionary, that's different, quite different," protested Mary.

"Is it?" asked George, raising his eyebrows. "Have you forgotten that you are married to a missionary, a Prussia Christian who has been sent by God to England?"

Mary opened her mouth, then closed it without saying a single word.

The next evening when George came home, the silverware, china, and tapestries were all gone. Sitting on the china cabinet in their place was a stack of pound notes. Mary pointed to them. "Do what you think best with it, George, and may God help us both," she said.

Only a week later George had another piece of disturbing news for his new wife. This time it concerned his salary. The Ebenezer Chapel paid George a generous salary of fifty-five pounds a year. Most of this money came from a practice called pew renting, whereby a person or family rented a particular church pew to sit in on Sundays. The richest people in the church rented the most expensive pews in the front, leaving the poor people to sit in the back pews, or "cheap seats," as they were known. It had been this way in the churches of England and Europe for hundreds of years, but the more George thought about it, the more wrong he decided the practice was. Church should not be a place where people were divided up according to how much money they had. There were no poor, second-class citizens in God's kingdom, and George did not see why there should be in the church on earth. Pew renting would have to go, and with it a good portion of the church's income and, in turn, a good portion of George's salary.

After dinner one evening in November, George and Mary Müller went for a walk along the seashore. The cockle and mussel sellers had gone home for the night, and the last few fishing boats were slipping into the harbor.

"Mary," said George gently, "thank you for selling the things. Now there is another matter we need to talk about."

Mary stopped and looked directly at her husband.

George took a deep breath before he went on. "It's the pew rent. I can't see how we can follow Jesus' command to treat all men equally as brothers if we give the rich people the best pews at the front of the church. In the Bible the book of James clearly tells us that we are not to show favor to rich people in the church, because that is dishonoring the poor."

After a long moment of silence, George heard Mary gasp. "But George, that's our only income…," Mary said, her voice trailing off.

"I know," he replied gently.

"You want me to say it's all right for you to give up our income?" she asked incredulously.

"Yes," said George frankly. "I know it's hard, but I think it is the right thing to do. The congregation should be free to give to us because God directs them to, not because they want the best pew in the church."

"But what if they don't want to give freely to us?" asked Mary.

"Well then, God will have to provide for us in another way," said George, reaching for his wife's hand. "Mary, do you think you can do it?"

Mary was silent for a long time as they continued to walk along the seashore. The only sounds were from the waves lapping against the seawall and the gulls squawking overhead.

Finally Mary spoke. "Do what you think is best, George. I can trust God, just like you do."

George stopped and hugged his wife. Tears spilled down his cheeks. Mary had been right—marriage had not become a prison for him. Instead, it had given him a partner in faith. "God will not let us down," he said with more confidence than he actually felt at that moment.

The next night after dinner, the two of them went out for another walk, this time in the opposite direction towards Ebenezer Street. When they reached the chapel, George unlocked it, and they both slipped inside. George lit the oil lamp at the back of the room and reached into the canvas bag he was carrying. He pulled out a wooden box about the size of a shoe box that had a slot cut in the top and a hinge door on the side. "Hand me a nail, Mary," he said in a determined voice. Within five minutes, the box was securely attached to the back wall.

"Do you have the sign?" he then asked Mary.

Mary nodded as she handed it to him.

After George had nailed the sign over the box, he stood back to admire his handiwork. "Yes," he said, squeezing his wife's hand. "We are at the mercy of God now." He scanned the sign and nodded. "Just like it says, Mary, if anyone wants to support us, they are welcome to. We will never ask anyone for money. Instead, we will look to God to supply our needs."

As the two of them knelt together beside a pew, they asked God to take care of them and give them the faith to keep to their new plan.

As George stepped outside, he grinned widely. He knew he had felt like this once before—when was it? He was halfway home before he recalled that it was the day he had told his father he would no longer accept any money from him for his studies at Halle University. He had that same feeling of freedom, of being dependent on God and not on people. The feeling excited George greatly.

Things did not work out quite as quickly, however, or as smoothly as they had at Halle. The year of 1831 was a trying one for the Müllers. Some members of the congregation continued to drop the same amount of money into the wooden box on the back wall as they had dropped into the offering plate. But many did not, probably because it was no longer "buying" them anything. Of course, this had a great impact on George's salary.

On one desperate occasion, George and Mary sat down at dinnertime to a table set with empty plates and nothing cooking in the oven. Undeterred,

George offered a prayer of thanks. As he prayed, there was a knock at the door. A friend in nearby Exmouth had sent a special delivery—a whole ham! George prayed an even greater prayer of thanks and then carved the ham so that he and Mary could eat. Another time, a total stranger had come to the door. When Mary opened it, she was met by a woman who gave her a curtsy. "I could not eat while I thought of you going hungry, ma'am," she said, handing Mary a freshly baked loaf of bread. Before Mary could ask her her name or where she was from, the woman had disappeared.

Often, when George was away preaching, the churches he visited would offer him money. George always refused it, saying he did not want to leave the impression he was preaching for money. Not to be put off, the churches found creative ways to "pay" their preacher. Sometimes George would find money stuffed into his Bible, or Mary, who often traveled with him, would find that someone had slipped coins into her purse while she was not looking.

All in all, by the end of the year, George and Mary had learned several things about trusting God. First, He did provide for them. They never missed a meal or had a need that was not met in some way. Second, to trust Him fully, they had to learn to give away any extra money they had. They never kept money they did not need and never allowed themselves to borrow a single penny, even if they had a need. They believed that God would provide exactly what they needed when they needed it. And He had.

In the spring of 1831, George thanked God for how well everything had turned out. He had come to Teignmouth sixteen months earlier with no job, little money, and one friend. Now he could not walk down the street without being stopped a dozen times to talk with friends. He had given up his salary of fifty-five pounds, and in return, God had provided food and rent money. He now had a wife who stood beside him, and in five months their first child would be born. The church congregation had grown to fifty-one members, many of them recent converts. Everything was going well for George in Teignmouth, except for one detail. George didn't think he belonged there anymore.

Chapter 7

A Mission Field Right Here

Bristol!" Mary Müller exclaimed. "Whatever makes you think we should move to Bristol? Can't we stay where we are, at least until the baby comes?" She brushed tears from her eyes as she spoke.

George put his arm around his wife. "Mary," he said gently, "I told you, and I told the whole congregation, that I would stay here only as long as God called me to."

"But George," Mary interrupted, "how can you be so sure?"

George was silent for a long moment. It was hard to explain, but the more he had prayed about it, the more he knew God was calling him northward to Bristol. Henry Craik was already living there, and he had written to George encouraging him to visit. In April 1832, George had taken him up on the offer.

Bristol was a bustling port city, second only to Liverpool in the number of ships it serviced. Like any other English city in the early nineteenth century, it was smoky and dirty. Beggars stood on the street corners, and small dirty children weaved though the crowds, no doubt looking for a purse to snatch or pocket to pick. Yet for all its crime and poverty, or rather because of it, George had felt that Bristol was a city he could work in, a city that needed plenty of help.

George and Henry Craik had held ten days of meetings at the Gideon and Pithay Chapels in the city. Each night was busier than the night before until, on April 29, Gideon Chapel was filled to overflowing. People sat on the stairs, others gathered outside the open windows, and still more crammed into the foyer at the back of the chapel. Many others had to be turned away because there was simply no more room anywhere for them.

After the meeting, many of the regular members of the congregation at Gideon Chapel begged George to move to Bristol. George and Henry Craik talked long into the night about it, finally drawing up a list of requirements that the congregation would need to agree to before George would even consider such a move. (1) George Müller and Henry Craik would not be traditional pastors, asking the congregation or board members what they thought best for them to do in every situation. Rather, they needed to be free to do whatever they felt God was calling them to do. (2) All pew rents were to be abolished, and neither man would be paid a salary. Together, the pastors and the congregation would trust God for enough money to run the chapel and meet all their needs. (3) George and Henry would be joint pastors, working together as a team, without one being the senior and the other the junior pastor.

George knew that these were not easy conditions for a church to meet, and when he received a letter from Henry Craik saying the congregation had agreed to all of them, he began to feel he should give serious consideration to moving to Bristol. As he prayed long and hard about it, deep down he knew it was indeed time to leave Teignmouth for Bristol.

Finally, Mary sighed. "Do what you think is best, George. I am sure I can have the baby just as well in Bristol as I could here, though I will miss all of my friends."

George had compasion for his wife. He had lived in many places, but she had been in Devon all her life. He knew it would be hard for her to make new friends, but he was sure he was doing the right thing.

"That's it, then," he concluded. "I'll start visiting everyone in the congregation tomorrow and tell them of our plans myself."

Two days and many tears later, George Müller had told everyone at Ebenezer Chapel that he was moving to Bristol.

It took less than an hour to pack their few belongings, and with sad hearts, on May 25, 1832, the Müllers boarded a stagecoach for Bristol. George was now twenty-six years old. As the stage rumbled along, he wondered what challenges lay ahead for him.

At first everything went smoothly. The Müllers and Henry Craik found a modest house with five bedrooms and two sitting rooms where they could live together. A rich Christian man had rented a second chapel, called Bethesda Chapel, and the two men divided services between it and Gideon Chapel. Meanwhile, Mary remained in good health, with the baby being due at the end of September.

It was the church bells, though, that first alerted George to the looming disaster in the city. The bells tolled after a funeral, and at the beginning of June, they began to toll almost nonstop. A cholera epidemic had descended on Bristol.

In nineteenth-century England, major differences existed between a city and a village. In villages people lived in their own cottages or in small groups of row houses. They drank water from their own wells and got rid of their bathroom waste in their gardens. In cities, Bristol included, things were much different. People lived in long rows of brick houses that snaked for miles without a single tree or field in sight. Dirty water and sewage overflowed from open drains that ran alongside the streets, and the water that was piped into houses was untreated and often carried germs and bacteria from polluted streams. These differences made conditions ripe for deadly diseases to spread in the city, and no disease was more feared than cholera.

Cholera spread like wildfire, killing thousands of people. George and Henry Craik were called out at all hours of the day and night to pray for those who had been stricken with the disease. Those who caught it usually died quickly. Often it took only twelve hours from the time a person first began to feel sick and started vomiting to the time he or she was laid in a coffin—that is, if a coffin could be found.

The work was exhausting, and it seemed like it would never end. All through July and August, bodies piled up on the sidewalks, waiting for carts to carry them away. Often they lay there rotting for a week or more because the cart driver himself had died of the disease and it was difficult to find someone brave enough to replace him.

Everyone knew that the best chance for staying healthy was to keep away from other people, especially large groups of people, where the disease could spread quickly. However, the folks at the two chapels wanted to continue meeting together to comfort and encourage one another. George and Henry agreed with them, and so they held a prayer meeting each morning to ask God to spare them and to stop the epidemic. Often two or three hundred people would ignore the risks of meeting together and show up to be led in prayer by George or Henry. Even though the people prayed earnestly, the church bells in the city continued to toll.

It was hard for George as he trudged from one end of Bristol to the other. The young pastor was welcomed into any house he stopped at. Even total strangers reached out to grab him as he walked by. George would read the Bible aloud to them and pray for the dying, or he would comfort a hysterical widow who now had no way to feed her ragged, hollow-cheeked children.

Mary Müller was fighting her own battle. Every morning she watched her husband walk out the door and into danger. Each time George reached out to hold the hand of a dying child or help a woman lay her husband's dead body out or hug a little child, he was exposing himself to cholera.

"What if you get sick?" Mary asked him. "Have you thought of that?"

George nodded silently. Of course, he had thought of it a thousand times. Every meal could easily be his last, especially given the number of people he touched who were dying. "But I have to do it, Mary. Somebody has to help these people and let them know God cares."

"And what about me?" Mary pleaded. "Does God care about me and our little one? There is nothing to guarantee you will even be alive to see it born." She wiped away the tears with the corner of her apron as she spoke.

"I know, I know," said George soothingly. "But Mary, you cannot imagine me hiding inside my own house while there are people who need God's comfort and the little I can do for them, can you?"

Mary shook her head. "No," she agreed quietly. "That would not be the man I married."

On September 16, George did stay home—all day—to assist the midwife with the birth of his baby daughter Lydia. In spite of all the death around them, Lydia was a thriving, healthy baby. By the time she was a month old, the cholera epidemic had finally run its course. A huge service of thanksgiving was held at Gideon Chapel. Of the two hundred people who regularly attended the two chapels, only one had died.

January 4, 1833, brought with it a blessing and a mystery. That morning George had collected the mail and noticed a letter postmarked from Baghdad. When he slit the envelope open, a check for two hundred pounds fell out. George quickly scanned the letter that came with it for some clue as to what the money was for. No one could have been more surprised than George when he read that the money was for him, his family, and Henry Craik to travel to Baghdad to be missionaries there. The letter writer promised more money would follow when they arrived.

Excitement stirred inside George. Was this the opportunity he had been waiting for since becoming a Christian? Had all of his time in England been training to prepare him to go and tell the lost souls in other lands about God? He hoped so. His brother-in-law Anthony Groves wrote regularly from Persia, and the life of a foreign missionary sounded so much more adventurous than that of a pastor in

England, making endless house calls and drinking bottomless cups of tea.

George hurried off to tell Henry Craik about the letter. Henry, too was excited. The two of them talked about it all morning, and by lunchtime they had all but convinced themselves they should both go to Baghdad.

After lunch, George had promised to visit a member of the congregation, a cobbler who lived about two miles away in the poorest part of Bristol. It had rained the night before. As he made his way there, George had to jump over muddy puddles, and every carriage that went by sprayed water up at him. George had just passed the bakery on Newfoundland Street when a little girl came up to him. She was no more than five years old, and she was piggybacking a toddler, a small boy with a runny nose and wearing only a torn pair of trousers.

"Please, mister," the little girl said with a lisp, "could you spare us a shilling? Me ma's gone with the cholera and me dad went to the mines and didn't come back."

George stopped and crouched beside the little girl. "What's your name, dear?" he asked, thinking of his own daughter tucked in her warm crib.

"Emily," she replied, "and I can spell it, too. Me ma taught me." Her eyes shone with delight from her dirt-streaked face.

"Can you now?" smiled George. "Well, I'll tell you what. You spell it correctly, and you will have earned your shilling."

"E-M-I-L-Y," she said triumphantly as she stuck out her grubby hand.

George laughed. "Perfect," he said reaching into his pocket. "Here's your shilling, and God bless you, Emily."

As Emily hitched her brother higher up her back and picked her way through the crowd, George felt strangely saddened. He had seen little girls and boys like Emily every day of the six months he'd lived in Bristol, but none of them had affected him like this. Where was Emily going? Did she have anywhere to sleep at night? Was a kind adult watching over her, or was she at the mercy of some evil person? What would happen to her brother if she got sick, or where would she go for help if he became ill?

These questions haunted George Müller, and as he walked along, he wondered why he had not seen it before. He didn't need to go to the mission field in Baghdad, or anywhere else for that matter. He was standing in the middle of a mission field! Surely there could be no more needy people in all the world than little children like Emily and her brother. Baghdad might sound foreign and exciting with its colorful bazaars, camels, and pipe music, but there was also work to be done in dirty, overcrowded Bristol. George did not know how to go about it or what a lone person with no regular income could do, but he knew one thing: with God's help, he would do something to help the poor homeless children of Bristol. "Yes," he said to himself aloud as he quickened his pace. "God has given me a mission field right here, and I will live and die in it."

Chapter 8

The Breakfast Club

"Where will they all sit?" asked Mary Müller as she stood in her living room lifting the heavy iron to press one of her husband's collars. Lydia, a serious little one-year-old toddler, scurried around her feet.

"I don't know," said George. "I was thinking of asking the grocer if he had any apple boxes he could spare. Tipped on their sides they'd make good seats, don't you think?"

Mary nodded vaguely. "I suppose so," she replied. "You really are determined to do this, aren't you?"

"Yes," replied George firmly. "There are children out on the streets of Bristol who have never heard the name of God, have never set foot in a church, and have no reason on this earth to hope. I have to do what little I can to help them. Right now the best I can do is invite them in for breakfast and read the Scriptures to them."

"But how many do you think will show up? Do you have a limit on how many we can feed?" asked Mary Müller, panic beginning to show on her face. "How is all this going to work, George? We hardly have enough breakfast for the three of us most of the time."

"If God is in this, He will supply," was George's reply.

And so the Breakfast Club began. Within a month of its start, twenty to thirty ragged children were gathered around the Müllers' steps each morning. At eight o'clock, George invited them in. Mary greeted them at the door. A pitcher of warm water was waiting on the counter inside, and the children took turns washing their faces and hands. Then they took their seats on the apple boxes that were placed around the oak table in the parlor. Mary ladled out a large helping of oatmeal to each child, and then George said grace. The children ate noisily while Mary poured them cups of strong tea. While the children shoveled spoonfuls of sugar into the tea, George began the Bible lesson. Sometimes he would read a story aloud to them, acting out the various parts as he went.

The popularity of the Breakfast Club grew, until a year later there was no room for even one more apple box in the Müllers' parlor. Forty people (not just children) showed up for breakfast every morning. Many adults needed food and Bible reading, and George knew there were hundreds if not thousands of other children in Bristol who needed a good breakfast and a Bible lesson, but he could not reach them all, at least not from inside his parlor. There had to be a way to do more, but how?

For days George paced the floor. He had something on his mind, something that would not go away. It was a name, a long name—the Scriptural Knowledge Institution for Home and Abroad. George could picture exactly what it would be: an organization run by Christian men like himself, an organization with three purposes: to establish day schools, Sunday schools, and adult schools for the poor; provide Bibles for people who could not afford to buy them; and help foreign missionaries with financial gifts. To accomplish these goals, George decided the organization would never ask a non-Christian for money or allow such a person to sit on its board. Nor would it go into debt of any kind. The success of the organization would be judged not by how much money it raised but rather by how it spent what it had.

With this all settled in his mind, George went to talk to Henry Craik, who agreed with all George outlined. A meeting was announced for March 5, 1834. About one hundred people came to listen to the two pastors as they outlined their idea for the Scriptural Knowledge Institution for Home and Abroad. Many people thought it was too bold, too far-fetched to ever become a reality.

Two weeks later, on March 19, Mary Müller gave birth to their second child, a son whom they named Elijah. Of course, the new arrival stretched the Müllers' finances, and by April, George had become very frustrated. Despite the public meeting and the hours George had spent praying and planning with Henry Craik, the Scriptural Knowledge Institution for Home and Abroad had not gotten off the ground. Not one penny had been raised for it, and George began to wonder whether he'd made a big mistake. He decided to pray a very specific prayer.

In his bedroom, George knelt beside his bed and prayed. "God, I believe You gave me the idea to start this organization, but I am not making any progress. If You want me to keep on with it, please send me twenty pounds to demonstrate this is Your will. I'll use the twenty pounds to buy Bibles to give away. Amen."

When he got up from his knees, George felt much better. The matter was in God's hands now, not his. If it succeeded, it would be because God had blessed it. If it failed, it would be because He had not.

That evening as the Müllers were sitting down to a meal of mutton stew, which seemed to contain more potatoes than meat, there was a knock at the door. When George opened the door, a woman from the Gideon Chapel stood before him.

"I'm sorry to bother you, sir," said the woman, curtsying, "but I had something on my mind, and I can get no rest from it. Here, take this, and God bless you." She thrust her hand into her coat pocket and pulled out a white envelope.

George reached out and took the envelope from the woman. The envelope felt like it had money in it, a pile of notes. The woman turned to walk down the steps.

"Wait a moment, please," said George. "I have a question for you."

The woman stopped. "What is it?" she asked as she turned around.

"I was wondering exactly what it was you wanted me to do with this."

"Well," she said, "whatever your need is."

George frowned. The woman sounded unsure. "But did you have something in particular you would like to see done with it?" he probed.

"Well, to be honest with you, if you don't need it urgently, I fancied the money going to buy Bibles for the poor." She gave a little smile.

"Thank you," said George, stepping down to grasp her hand. "Thank you a hundred times."

As George closed the door and walked back into the parlor, Mary looked up at him. "What is it, George?" she asked.

"An answer to my prayer," he said, his face shining with joy. "If I'm not mistaken, this envelope should contain twenty pounds." He tore it open, and sure enough, four five-pound notes fell out.

"Oh, Mary!" he exclaimed. "God is in this after all. We had better get ready. I know He is about to open the floodgates!"

And open they did. Within six months of receiving the first gift, the Scriptural Knowledge Institution for Home and Abroad was providing education for one hundred twenty children in Sunday school and two hundred children and forty adults in day school. One thousand Bibles had been purchased and given away, and fifty-seven pounds had been sent overseas for the support of missionaries. George accounted for every halfpenny of the money in his meticulous records. Everything was recorded, from the principal's salary to the coal for the heaters, the chalk for the blackboard, and cricket balls for sports day.

For the next year, things proceeded well for the Müllers. George was still pastor of Gideon and Bethesda Chapels, he continued giving free breakfasts to poor children, he oversaw the day schools and Sunday schools, and in his spare time he looked forward to being with his own two children—Lydia, who was now two, and baby Elijah. But in June 1835, tragedy struck the family. Elijah, now fifteen months old, became sick with influenza. George had visited enough sick children to know that his son was in grave danger. He wrote in his journal, "[May] the Lord's holy will be done concerning the dear little one." The next day Elijah died. It was a very difficult time for George, who missed his son terribly. But it was an even more difficult timed for Mary. Four days earlier, her father, whom she had been close to, had died. Now she was left with two funerals to arrange and attend in a single week.

Later that same year, ill health crept up on George. George had never quite fully recovered from his stomach hemorrhage, and the old problem flared up again. Mary feared that her husband might die on her as well. The doctor made it clear to George that he needed a change of air if he was to have any hope of recovery. So with Mary and Lydia, George traveled to the Isle of Wight, where he spent his thirtieth birthday.

For once, George had time to read, and he took advantage of it. He read the biographies of many great missionaries, including John Newton. He also took time to read various newspapers. Each day the consequences of the Poor Law Amendment Act seemed to make the headlines, and George could see why. Until 1834, the English government, through church parishes, had helped to support working people during times when they were unable to find a job. This support had kept many families from starving, and allowed men the dignity of returning to work as soon as they could find it. However, in 1834, that had all changed. In an effort to save money, the government had taken away the support it provided for the working poor and replaced it with a policy stating that a family that could not support itself would have to go to a poorhouse.

Even as George convalesced on the Isle of Wight, many new poorhouses were being built around the country. Poorhouses were awful places, and they were meant to be. The government wanted them to be as unattractive as possible to discourage people from applying. But without the extra financial support from the government, hundreds of working families, single parents, and orphans had nowhere else to turn, no matter how unattractive the poorhouses were made to be.

The more George read about these places, the sadder he became. Husbands, wives, and children in the poorhouses were all separated and made to do the most menial work. For twelve or fourteen hours a day, people were forced to crush horse and cow bones by hand, break rocks apart, and hand-grind corn. After a day's work, they flopped exhausted onto their lice- and flea-infested bunks, knowing they would have to get up the next day and do it all over again. In return for their labor, workers got two meals a day, to be eaten in silence. All children seven years old and up were made to work and were not allowed to see their parents, even if they were in the same poorhouse. The death rate in the poorhouses was high. Disease flourished in the horrid living conditions, and such a sense of hopelessness hung in the air that many people committed suicide.

Every day on the Isle of Wight, George prayed for Henry Craik and the ongoing work in Bristol, where he longed to be. With the growing poorhouse situation, there was going to be more work than ever.

As soon as George got better, he returned to Bristol. On November 15, he wrote in his diary, "We arrived safely. Last week we prayed repeatedly concerning the work of the Scriptural Knowledge

Institution and especially that the Lord will give us the means to continue and even enlarge the work."

Within a short time of George's return to Bristol, three events occurred, any one of which was interesting, but when put together, they convinced George that it was time to begin the work for which he would come to be known around the world.

The principal of the boys' school run by the Scriptural Knowledge Institution came to report on the school's progress. George knew each student in the school. He knew his likes and dislikes and what he hoped to be when he grew up. As a result, George was very interested in what the principal had to say. Since each student represented a hope for the future, George was upset when he learned that Freddie, one of the first boys to enroll, and a good student, had been taken to the poorhouse. Children had fewer rights than anyone else in the poorhouse. Freddie would not be allowed visitors unless the matron approved them, he could not leave the poorhouse to go to school, and he could not own any private property, not even the Bible George had given him.

George lay his head in his hands. "Why did it have to happen to Freddie?" he asked, directing his question at no one in particular.

The principal responded. "It seems his father was dragged off to jail, for petty theft, I think, and he died there the same night. His mother was taken by cholera, and his aunt took care of him. She waited until there was not a scrap of food left in the house, and then she marched Freddie down to the poorhouse so he could at least eat."

"It's so unfair," replied George. "What good is it opening schools if the children can't come because they have no food and no lodging?"

The question hung in the air, and George was still trying to work out an answer to it when he visited Bill Wentworth, a member of the congregation at Gideon Chapel. Bill Wentworth pumped the bellows for the forge at one of the new factories that were springing up all over Bristol. Indeed, George was actually surprised to find him home, since Bill Wentworth seemed to be at work all the time.

"Hello, Mr. Wentworth, may I come in?" called George through the open doorway.

"Of course you can. Make yourself comfortable, and I'll have the missus put on a pot of tea for us," said Bill Wentworth, wiping his hands on a dirty rag. "What can I do for you then?"

"I was just in the neighborhood and thought I'd visit. I'm surprised to catch you at home," replied George.

Bill Wentworth nodded grimly. "Yeah, I'm glad for the job, don't make any mistake about that, but the hours are awful long. Normally, I work sixteen hours a day, sometimes longer." He coughed hard when he stopped talking.

"And do you have time for prayer and Bible study?" George asked.

Bill Wentworth looked sheepish. "Not really. By the time I'm done with work, I'm not much good for anything but sleep, to be honest."

"Have you thought of working less? You don't sound too healthy," said George.

Bill Wentworth laughed scornfully. "If you don't mind me saying so, it's all very well to say what we should be doing from the pulpit, it's quite another to have to earn a living for your family. Why, if I didn't work all the time, the whole family would be dragged off to the poorhouse, and we all know what that's like!"

George nodded. Many in his congregation had told him they worked such long hours that there was simply no time left for spiritual things. Still, George was not ready to give up on Bill Wentworth. "You have to understand that God has promised to supply the needs of all His children. Jesus told us to seek God's kingdom first and He will add all the other things to us."

"It's a fine idea, Pastor, but if I cut back on my hours, I don't think God would provide real things for me like shoes or food, do you?" Bill Wentworth looked a little embarrassed. "I mean, I know the Bible says He can do that, and you preach it and all. But I've never seen it for myself, in real life, if you know what I mean."

Again George nodded. He did know what Bill Wentworth meant, only too well. He had heard the same argument a hundred times before. Yes, the person believed that God could provide for him, but no, he was not prepared to take time out of his overworked life to pray and serve others and allow God to meet his needs. George longed for something or someone to point to, something he could show a person and say, "Look, he honored God, and God is looking after him in every way."

Several days after visiting Bill Wentworth, George visited another member of the congregation. Unlike Bill, Elizabeth Brinsdon had a lot of spare time. And judging from her collection of books, George figured she must spent a lot of it reading. He sat in a well-padded chair chatting away with Elizabeth Brinsdon as a servant poured tea for them.

"Please, have a scone," Elizabeth Brinsdon offered, holding out a fine china plate with five scones neatly arranged on it. Each scone was spread with bright red raspberry jam with a dollop of Devonshire cream on top.

"Thank you," said George. "These look delicious. I see you have a great many interesting books. Do you mind if I look?"

"By all means," replied Elizabeth Brinsdon. "And if any of them interest you, feel free to borrow them."

George put down his cup of tea and scone and stood to scan the bookshelf nearest him. Many of the books he had studied at school and at university. There were also ancient Greek and Latin texts, as well as some books by new English novelists. George reached up to pull out a small, dark, leather-bound book that had no name on its spine.

"You might be interested in that book, Pastor. If I remember correctly, it was translated from German," Elizabeth Brinsdon said as George lifted the book from the shelf.

Goosebumps ran up and down George's neck as he turned the book over and read its title. The volume was an English translation of the biography of A. H. Franke, the professor from Halle University who had started the orphanage in Halle.

"Do you know the book?" asked Elizabeth Brinsdon.

"As a matter of fact, I do," George replied. "When I was a university student at Halle, I stayed in a room at the orphanage he started."

Elizabeth Brinsdon's eyes sparkled. "Then you must take the book, Pastor Müller. I'm sure you will want to reacquaint yourself with the wonderful story."

George lay in bed that night unable to sleep. He thought about Bill Wentworth and all the men and women he was constantly encouraging to trust God. What or who was it that he could point to to help them understand what he was talking about? He thought of Freddie, who at that very moment was alone in a room filled with men, some kind, some mentally ill, and some just plain evil. And he thought of the biography of A. H. Franke. How strange it was to find it in a private library in Bristol, England.

"Somehow," George prayed, "let me be a light to those around me, and help me to find a way to reach the orphans before it's too late."

In his wildest dreams, George Müller could not have imagined how his simple prayer would be answered.

Chapter 9

The First Orphanage in Bristol

The Wednesday night two weeks before Christmas was cold and windy. George and Mary Müller walked arm in arm up Paul Street from their home towards Gideon Chapel on their way to a special meeting. When they arrived, they found the chapel already crowded with people. They made their way to the front of the chapel. As George stood to speak, he could feel his heart thumping wildly with excitement and anticipation. He cleared his throat and began the speech that was to be the outline for the rest of his life's work. "I have called this meeting for one purpose," he began. "God has told me to start an orphanage."

The audience let out a gasp and murmured as George went on to tell them about the pattern of operation for his orphanage. There would be no collections, no asking for money, and no payment required from the children who were taken in. Instead, George would rely on God to supply all the needs of the orphans.

After he had finished talking, George invited questions from the audience. Some were practical, such as, Where was the orphanage to be located? George did not know, since God had not yet shown him a house. What orphans would he take in, and how many? George thought there would probably be around thirty girls aged seven to twelve. How old would a girl be when she left the orphanage? George wasn't sure. He hoped to find work for most of the girls as domestic servants when they were twelve, but no girl would be returned to the streets because she was too old for the orphanage. Some place would be found for her to go. Did he have any staff? Not yet.

Some of the questions were more spiritual. One man with a long gold watch chain draped across his ample belly asked if George really thought God was interested in the daily needs of an orphanage. Did he honestly think, for instance, that God would send chamber pots and bandages, schoolbooks and socks for thirty girls whom no one loved or cared about? George replied that they would have to wait and see, but in his experience, there wasn't anything too large or small to ask God for.

When the questions were finished, George concluded the meeting in prayer, and then he made his way to the back of the chapel to greet people on their way out. There he heard all of the comments people had not wanted to make in front of others.

"I do think it's a big project to take on," said one elderly woman. "I think if God is calling you to work with orphans, you might be better to take one or two into your home. It doesn't do to bite off more than you can chew. Besides, if the orphanage failed, it would be an embarrassment to us all," she told George, patting him soothingly on the arm.

"I've never heard of such a thing," muttered another man as he put on his hat and coat. "I don't see how it could possibly work. The poorhouse is the best place for an orphan. Can't get into any mischief there."

"If you were an Englishman, Mr. Müller," began another woman in a proud voice, "you would know this type of thing is not possible in England. It is not the way we do things here. Perhaps asking God to supply all your needs is the way things are done in Prussia, but not here."

George looked her in the eye. "I believe God is our provider wherever we live," he said kindly, thinking to himself that this was one of the reasons he was starting the orphanage—to show people that God does indeed provide.

But for every negative comment there was a positive one to counterbalance it. One woman pressed a ten-shilling note into George's hand and said, "I will pray for you every day, Pastor Müller. May God guide you."

Another woman stood squarely in front of George, and looking him right in the eye, she said, "I'm not much with book learning, sir. But I know how to cook and clean, and goodness knows, I've mended a thousand socks in my day. If you can use me in your new orphanage, I'm ready to be put to work. And don't worry about paying me. The good Lord's never let me starve yet, and I don't thinks He's about to now. If you can have faith for those thirty girls, I can have faith for myself."

"God bless you, and thank you," said George, shaking her hand. "You are just the type of person we need. Come to my house tomorrow and we will talk."

The woman nodded and waved good-bye as she walked out the door.

As George and Mary walked home, they talked about the meeting. Despite the negative comments, it had been a good evening in many ways. George had known that some people would disagree with his plan. But he also knew that some people, like the woman who had offered to cook and clean for the girls, would be in favor of it. Those people were an inspiration.

The next morning, the local newspaper printed a small article about the meeting under the headline "Local Minister Intends to Set Up Orphanage." The article said that if George succeeded, it would be the first orphanage in Bristol. In fact, according to the newspaper, there were only ten or twelve orphanages in the whole of England. And all but one of them were private orphanages, taking only "children whose parents had been of some means, but now found themselves without sufficient funds to care entirely for their own needs." The London Orphan Asylum, for example, insisted that children of domestic or agricultural servants and children of journeymen tradesmen would not be eligible. On top of this, children with any medical problems, diseases, or deformities were not accepted. George was glad he had made it clear that the new orphanage would not turn away any child in need as long as there was space for the child.

Later that same day, George received a letter. He frowned as he turned it over and saw that the postmark was from a town one hundred miles north of Bristol. He could not think of anyone he knew there. He opened the letter and began to read.

"Mary, Mary," he yelled, "come and listen to this!"

Mary came out of the kitchen, wiping her hands on her apron. "What is it, George?" she asked, surprised.

"This letter is from a married couple. Listen to what it says." He cleared his throat and began to read. "We offer ourselves to the service of the intended orphanage if you think us qualified for it."

"Oh, George," gasped Mary, "however did they know? You only announced it last night. Now, counting the housekeeper, we have three possible workers!"

"Wait, Mary, there's more," said George as he read on. "Also we would give up all the furniture, etc., which the Lord has given us, for its use. And we would do this without receiving any salary whatsoever, believing that if it be the will of God to employ us, He will supply all our needs."

"Isn't it wonderful, George," said Mary, grasping her husband's hands. "Everything is happening so quickly."

In a way it was. Yet in another way, George had been preparing for this for many years, ever since the day he had trusted God to supply his needs at Halle University.

George answered the couple immediately and accepted their offer, though he did tell them the orphanage didn't yet have a house or anything to put in it except what the couple brought with them. No sooner had he mailed the letter, than household items began arriving at his home. One man, who had been at the meeting the night before, had collected things from his neighbors to give to the orphanage: four knives and five forks, one jug, four mugs, three salt stands, three dishes, three basins, and twenty-eight plates.

After the man left, George scooped three-year-old Lydia into his arms. "You see, little one, God will supply all our needs according to His riches in glory," he said, as much to himself as to her. Lydia giggled as he whirled her around and around the parlor.

George continued to pray over the next week, and the things the orphanage needed flowed in. Blankets, money, fabric for the young girls' nightgowns, tablecloths, pillowcases, sheets, more basins, plates, and silverware arrived at the house almost hourly. George kept a careful record of every item and every penny that was donated.

After dinner on December 17, 1835, George sat at his desk and pulled out his black leather-bound journal. Lydia played at his feet as he dipped his pen into the inkwell and wrote: "This evening another brother brought a clothes horse, three frocks, four pinafores, six handkerchiefs, three counterpanes, one blanket, two pewter salt cellars, six tin cups, and six metal teaspoons. He also brought three shillings and sixpence given to him by three different individuals. At the same time, he told me that it had been put in the heart of an individual to send tomorrow one hundred pounds."

The next afternoon, the same man returned with more items, including sixteen thimbles, an iron, a sugar basin, four combs, and the one hundred pounds promised. He counted the money out for George. But instead of being happy to receive it, George was troubled when he heard who had given it—a poor spinster who lived in a boarding house. George knew that the woman made only about three shillings and sixpence a week by taking in hand sewing jobs. It would have taken her twelve years to earn the one hundred pounds!

All night, George tossed and turned thinking about the spinster. Where had she got the money? What would happen to her if she needed it later? Did she understand what she was doing? Was she being overly emotional instead of first thinking it through? By the following morning, George knew what he had to do. He neatly folded the one hundred pounds and slipped it into his vest pocket. "Mary," he called as he stood at the door, "I have to make a visit. I should be back in an hour or so."

Within fifteen minutes, George was knocking at the door of the spinster's boarding house. When he inquired whether she was in, the housekeeper invited him to make himself comfortable in the drawing room while she went to fetch her.

A minute or two after he'd sat down on the couch, the spinster entered the room. "I hope you don't mind me bringing my sewing. I got a bit behind last night," she said as George stood to greet her.

"Not at all," replied George. "I will not keep you. I came to ask you a simple question. Would you reconsider the gift you gave the orphanage? One hundred pounds is a lot of money to anyone, but for you, well...," he struggled to think of the right way to say it. "If God blessed you with the money, perhaps He intended you to keep it in case there is a time when you need it." He pulled the notes from his pocket. "It was a very generous gift, but I do not want to take advantage of your generosity."

George smiled apologetically as he placed the money on the table between them.

"But Mr. Müller," began the spinster, laying her needlework in her lap, "you don't understand. I want to give that money. I got an inheritance of four hundred and eighty pounds from my father. I gave my mother one hundred pounds, and the new orphanage one hundred pounds. The rest I used to pay off my father's debts. I am perfectly happy about what I've done with the money."

"Maybe you don't understand," said George, feeling he was getting nowhere. How could he take money from someone this poor?

"Now Mr. Müller, I don't want to contradict you, but I believe I do understand," the woman said very seriously. "The Lord Jesus gave His last drop of blood for me, and should I not give all the money I have for Him? In fact, I have five pounds over, and I have decided to give that to you as well, for you to share with the poorest members at the chapel."

George's eyes swam with tears. He knew he could say nothing but thank you. He had come to the boarding house to find answers, and he had found them. The spinster was giving the money because she wanted to, and not because she felt manipulated into it by anything or anyone. "Thank you," George said as he left the room. "I don't say thank you just for myself, because you have not given the money to me. You have given it to the orphans of Bristol. May God bless your generosity."

The spinster nodded. "I only hope God will allow me to give more before I die," she said.

On his way home, George stopped outside a large three-story house on Wilson Street, not far from Gideon Chapel. A member of the congregation had told him it had just come up for rent, and George was anxious to see it. The house was number six in a long row of identical houses. Each house was made of brick, had six windows, two on each floor, and had the same wooden eaves. As George cupped his hands against the front windowpane and peered inside, he heard a voice behind him. "Interested in the house, sir? It's for rent, you know."

George stepped back and turned around. He looked into the eyes of a tall, well-dressed man. "I can show you inside if you would like," the man offered.

"Thank you," said George. "I'd appreciate that."

Inside, the house was roomier than George had imagined. It had three bedrooms upstairs and a large living room on the middle floor, and the stove in the kitchen on the ground floor was big enough to cook for two families. The house was perfect, and by the time George left it, he had agreed to rent it. He hurried home to tell Mary. It was almost too good to be true. He had one hundred five pounds in his pocket, and he now had a house to run the orphanage in. And by the time he got home, he had an opening date in mind as well: February 3, 1836.

Chapter 10

An Orphanage on Wilson Street

On the morning of February 3, 1836, George Müller hurried to number six Wilson Street. In spite of the icy sleet falling, he was humming to himself as he walked. Today was the day the orphanage opened, and he could hardly believe how quickly everything had come together. It had been only seven weeks since he had stood in Gideon Chapel and announced his intention to start the orphanage. He remembered how some church members had told him it couldn't be done. He was glad that today those members were going to see that God does indeed answer prayer and that things that seem impossible to men are possible to Him.

As he turned the brass key in the lock and stepped inside, George was deeply thankful for everything he saw. The tables and chairs in the parlor, the blue velvet couch, the rose-colored rug, the chests of drawers upstairs filled with stacks of neatly folded underwear, petticoats, and socks, the cupboards with rows of shoes, the linen closet piled high with blankets and pillowcases—every single item was an answer to prayer. Even the house itself had been rented with donated money that was an answer to prayer. Since he had begun the adventure of starting the orphanage, George had kept a careful prayer diary. Down one side of each page in his diary he had recorded each prayer request, and on the other side, the date and the way in which it was answered. Every item in the house was on the list. Even the coal, which he began shoveling into the fireplace to warm the house, was an answer to prayer.

George washed his hands and dried them on a towel in the kitchen. Then he walked into the parlor and took a stack of papers from his bag. The papers were forms he had picked up from the printer the day before, forms for the guardians of the orphans to fill out. They asked for the child's full name, birth date, age, and education; date of the child's parents' death; and a person to contact in an emergency. As George had been drawing up the forms, he was aware that many of them would never be filled out completely. Some children as young as two or three years old wandered around alone. If some caring person or policeman brought one of them to the orphanage someday, it would be something if the child could remember his or her first name, let alone all the other information. Still, George reminded himself, today he couldn't accept applications from children that young even though he wanted to. For now, the orphanage was set up only for girls aged seven to twelve. He hoped that they or a guardian would be able to fill out more of the information.

George laid the forms out around the table so that several people could work on them at once. He knew many of the girls would be unable to read or write, but he hoped they would bring someone with them who could.

By lunch time, George had rearranged the forms five or six times as he waited for a knock at the door. The attic walls needed to be painted, but he hated to go upstairs and get up to his elbows in paint, because the girls would be arriving at the door at any moment, or so he told himself. But the girls did not arrive.

By five o'clock that night, not a single orphan had arrived at the fully equipped orphan house. The new "house parents" had been by several times to see whether anyone had shown up, and since no one had, they left for the day. The beds that George had expected little girls would be climbing into sat untouched, their bedspreads unruffled.

George was not humming when he walked home that evening. In his mind he reviewed the past seven weeks. What had gone wrong? Had he become too proud of what he was doing? Was that why God did not entrust a single child to him?

Hadn't he prayed hard enough? Was the whole idea of a free orphanage for needy children just too far-fetched? Were the naysayers right after all? George did not know the answers, and by the time he swung open the door to his own house, his heart was heavy.

Mary rushed to meet him, with Lydia not far behind. "Tell me all about it," she said, her face beaming with an expectant smile. "What are their names? How many are there? How old are they?"

George shook his head as he took off his coat and scarf. He sat down heavily in a chair. "There aren't any," he said with a sigh.

Mary frowned. "What do you mean, George? There aren't any what?"

"Any orphans," he replied flatly.

The smile evaporated from Mary's face and was replaced by a horrified look. "You mean not a single girl came?" she questioned.

George nodded. "Not a single one," he answered, and then he added, "Maybe this was all a mistake after all."

Mary walked over to her husband and put her hands on her hips in a determined stance. "How can you say that, George Müller? Look at all the prayers God has answered for us! Isn't the house an answer to prayer? Look how much money has been provided. Isn't that an answer to prayer, too? And the calico, the dishes, the furniture, everything in that house is an answer to prayer, and we both know it."

George lifted his head and looked at her for the first time since entering the house. "I know," he shrugged. "But there aren't any orphans, and that's not an answer to prayer, is it Mary?"

With that Mary clapped her hands together and laughed out loud.

Startled, George stared up at her. This was no time to be making fun. Couldn't she see that?

"But George," she said, her shining eyes wrapped up in a broad smile, "that's the whole point. We never did pray for children. Don't you see? We prayed for coal and food and paint and workers, but we never thought to pray for children!"

George was laughing now. "Mary, you are quite right. I didn't think we needed to because there are so many orphans on the streets, and I was sure we'd have applications from more people than we could house!" He caught his wife by the waist and swung her around. "Let's go and pray, Mrs. Müller," he said.

For the second morning in a row, George hummed as he walked to Wilson Street. This time he felt sure the orphan girls would come. After all, he had asked God to send them. And send them He did! The first children applied that day. By the end of the month, the orphanage housed twenty-six girls, and forty-two more were on the waiting list. It was April 2 before George found the time to organize an official opening ceremony.

Hundreds of people came to see the orphanage and to listen to Henry Craik preach at the official opening. George thanked the many hundreds of people who had helped make the orphanage a reality. Some, he pointed out, had helped in large ways, such as with the ton of coal that had been delivered to the house one day and the anonymous gift of one hundred pounds that had arrived the next day. But many of the gifts had been small, yet they meant just as much both to the person who had given them and to George, who told how a small boy who looked like he could have been an orphan himself knocked boldly on his door the day before, a shilling held tightly in his hand. "This is for your girls," the boy said when George opened the door. "I found a ring, and when I returned it to the owner, she gave me a shilling for being so honest. Here it is." A woman in Bristol sent George five shillings with a note saying she had gone to buy a new dress and deliberately chose the plainest one she could find rather than the more elaborate and expensive kind she normally purchased. The five shillings represented the money she had saved by purchasing the less expensive dress, and she wanted the orphanage to have it.

The year rushed by at a hectic pace. Besides having thirty girls to care for, George was still pastor of Gideon Chapel, which was growing rapidly, and he had not eased off in his efforts with the Scriptural Knowledge Institution for Home and Abroad. Three hundred fifty boys and girls were now in school, and the teachers' salaries, rents for the classrooms, and books were all provided by the institution. It seemed that the more responsibilities George took on, the more he was able to carry.

Although George never asked for help with the orphan girls, offers poured in. A local doctor offered to treat the girls for free, and George's old church at Teignmouth sent supplies and money to help. Housekeepers, laundry maids, and matrons either volunteered their services or agreed to work for lower wages than they could earn elsewhere.

Most people would have thought the hardest thing about starting an orphanage was raising the money, but for George Müller, the hardest thing was turning away needy children. The orphanage was not set up for boys or girls under seven years of age. It upset George greatly to have to tell a child or the child's temporary guardian that he was unable to help. So, even though he told no one, from the day of the official opening of the orphanage at number six Wilson Street, a plan had been taking shape in George's mind. According to his plan there would be a second orphanage and a third until every orphan in Bristol was being taken care of, taught to read, and told about God.

In October, George felt it was time to start putting his plan into action. He rented a second house, located at number one Wilson Street. The house was ideal in many ways. While it was an exact replica of the number six house and all the other houses in the long row that ran along Wilson Street, number one was at the beginning of the row and had an empty corner lot beside it. George managed to rent both the house and the adjoining lot. By the end of November, the house had been outfitted with cribs and rocking horses, and the lot had been turned into a playground for both orphanages. On November 28, 1836, the orphanage at number one Wilson Street was opened for business. Some of the older girls from the other orphanage helped with the babies and toddlers at the new one. Many of the girls would be going into domestic service as nannies, and the younger children gave them someone to practice their skills on, though a matron was always watching to make sure the babies were bathed and played with properly.

The week leading up to Christmas was a happy one for the Müller family, and especially happy for the children in the orphanages. The children's eyes shone with delight as they asked George how many more days there were to go and what they would be having for Christmas dinner. George loved to tease them and tell them he had forgotten all about Christmas. Of course, he hadn't. He knew it would be the first real Christmas for many of the children, and he prayed that God would make it memorable for them.

Christmas *was* memorable. All sorts of wonderful and delicious things were brought to the orphanage by the people of Bristol. Turkeys and ducks hung in the laundry room ready to be cooked. An enormous drum containing one hundred pounds of treacle sat in the corner of the kitchen, its top slightly askew where some of the children had already tasted its thick, sweet contents. Oranges and bananas from a shipment that had arrived in port from the West Indies were sent to the orphanage, and many church women made new Sunday clothes for the girls.

As George gathered his family, sixty orphan children, the orphanage staff, and Henry Craik for Christmas dinner, he could not help but smile with pure joy. He wondered what the policemen in Wolfenbüttel would think of him now. It had been fifteen Christmases ago that he'd sat in a cold, bare prison cell there after being captured trying to leave town without paying the innkeeper for his room. If George could have seen then what he was to become, he would never have believed it. God had taken George Müller, the boy who cared for no one but himself, and turned him into a man now responsible for the lives of dozens of orphan children. What a journey it had been, and George could not help but wonder where he would be and what he would be doing at Christmases to come.

Chapter 11

Food for the Children

The King Is Dead, Long Live the Queen," read the headline of the Tuesday, June 20, 1837, edition of the *Bristol Times*. George already knew what had happened, as did nearly everyone in Bristol. The news had traveled fast; all flags had been lowered to half-mast, shops were closed, and church bells tolled endlessly. That night after dinner, George and Mary Müller spent a long time praying for the new, eighteen-year-old queen, Victoria. Lydia, on the other hand, wanted to know what all the fuss was about. "Why don't the church bells stop ringing, Papa?" she asked. "Are they stuck?"

"No, my dear," replied George, hoisting her onto his lap. "King William IV died this morning, and many people are sad."

"He must have been very important," said Lydia.

"He was," George replied, "and people in England are sad. But on Saturday, everyone is going to be happy, and we will have the biggest parade you have ever seen. We will be celebrating a new queen. Her name is Queen Victoria, and she is only thirteen years older than you."

Lydia giggled at the thought.

That Saturday Lydia was at the parade with her parents and about forty of the older orphan children. All the people were given a Union Jack to wave as they watched the long procession of mayors, magistrates, and ministers go by in their carriages.

After the parade, George hurried home. He still had a lot of work to do if he was going to open a boys' orphanage at number three Wilson Street by the end of the month. Need for the new orphanage, which would house about forty boys, had become urgent, since there was nowhere else to send the little boys from the infant house when they turned seven years old.

The third orphan house opened on time, and George was now responsible for eighty-one children and nine full-time staff. The waiting list of children wanting to get into the orphanage was long enough to fill three more homes. Besides tending to the orphans, George, through the Scriptural Knowledge Institution for Home and Abroad, was providing an education for three hundred fifty children in day schools and another three hundred twenty in Sunday schools.

Later that year, George waited for the first copies of the book he had written, *Narrative of Some of the Lord's Dealings with George Müller,* to roll off the printing press. It had not been an easy decision to publish a book about what he had learned so far in his Christian life. In fact, George prayed more about publishing the book than about any other decision he'd made in his life. The last thing he wanted to do was to make himself look more important or give the impression that he had more faith than other Christians. But so many people had written to him asking for advice on how to lead a simple life of faith that in the end, he decided to write it down in a book.

The book sold briskly, and more than ever, George was asked to speak in other churches. It was not possible for him to accept these invitations, however, for one simple reason: George Müller was a very sick man. His health had deteriorated again, and he began to suffer from terrible headaches. The only temporary relief he seemed to find from them was to tie a handkerchief very tightly around his head. Sometimes he was forced to lie in bed for days on end. Over the next several months, he spent a great deal of time in other parts of the country, mostly staying with friends in the countryside, trying to recover. It worked a little.

In March 1838, George decided to return to Prussia for a visit. He hoped the change of air would do him good and provide the relief from sickness he sought. He also wanted to use the trip to encourage

German missionaries. He made the trip alone, leaving Mary behind to run the orphanage, which she in fact had been doing for most of the previous year.

George left England on April 2, 1838. The trip across the English Channel was rough, and George quickly added seasickness to his list of ailments. Still, he arrived safely in Hamburg on April 9 and made his way to Berlin, where he spent ten days meeting with missionaries. From Berlin he went to Heimersleben to visit his father. The two of them now got along much better than they had when George was at Halle University. Johann Müller was interested in all his son was doing in England. He also wanted to know how the young Queen Victoria was getting along. After all, the queen's mother was a German princess.

After a month away, as George made his way back to Bristol, he realized he had been right about the change of air. He felt much better. In fact, although he got sick from time to time, he never again experienced long, drawn out bouts of sickness such as the one he had just suffered through.

It was just as well George didn't stay away for too long, because things were rapidly becoming difficult back in Bristol. On August 18, 1838, George wrote in his journal, "I have not one penny in hand for the orphans. In a day or two again many pounds will be needed. My eyes are on the Lord."

By the end of that day, five pounds had arrived, a gift from a woman who had sold some of her jewelry for the benefit of the orphans. It was enough money to buy food for a day, but by evening, they were back in the same situation. On August 20, George again received a gift of five pounds, which was also used to buy food. The next day it was twelve pounds, and three pounds the following day.

Again and again, George added up the books, only to find that the orphan houses did not have a penny for food. Each time he prayed, money arrived in the nick of time. Given the pressing need, there was a temptation to use other money to meet it, but George stood firm. On one occasion a check for two hundred twenty pounds arrived from a wealthy landowner in the area. The cover letter with the check said the money was for the Scriptural Knowledge Institution for Home and Abroad. George knew that all he had to do was to ask whether it could be used for the orphans and the wealthy landowner would immediately agree. But George would not ask. He wanted nothing to do with manipulating circumstances. God had promised to provide for them all, and George would continue to pray and believe that. He would not take money that had been given for one thing and use it for something else.

Another time, George received a large sum of money from a woman he knew was in debt. From the day he became a Christian, George hated debt. He believed that if God intended someone to have something, He would provide the money beforehand to buy it, not afterwards. Because of this, he knew he could not keep the woman's donation. Even though he did not have enough money for food the next day, he sent the money back and suggested the woman use it to pay her creditors instead. The next day, as it always did, enough money arrived to pay for the daily supplies of the orphan houses.

On one occasion, George managed to unintentionally insult a woman who had come to give him a large sum of money. The woman's name was Mrs. Brightman. One day when George arrived home from the Wilson Street orphan homes, he found Mrs. Brightman drinking tea in the parlor with Mary. After Mary introduced her, George sat down and joined in the conversation, which quickly turned to the ways in which God provided for the orphans. Mrs. Brightman seemed interested in everything George said, and as George looked at her, he was sure he knew why. Mrs. Brightman was a tiny woman, dressed in clothes that were too thin for a November day, and her boots were all but worn through. George was sure she wanted to know the secret to God's provision for her own life. The more they talked, the more sorry George felt for her.

Abruptly, Mrs. Brightman said, "Well, I have to go now. You'll be wanting to get your dinner on the table. Thank you for your time."

George looked at Mary, who promptly spoke. "But Mrs. Brightman, we would be honored if you would stay and have dinner with us. You have so many questions, and we are enjoying your company."

"No, I wouldn't hear of it. I can't impose on you good folk any longer. I'll be off now. Besides, I have a train to catch, not that I'll be able to eat anything they serve. Get me my shawl if you would be so kind, Mrs. Müller. It's the only one I have, and I don't mean to leave it behind."

Something stirred inside George as he watched Mary go to get Mrs. Brightman's shawl. Mrs. Brightman was such a thin woman, out there in the cold with only a shawl to keep her warm. And what was that she had said about not eating anything on the train? She had come all this way and didn't even have enough money for a piece of pie? As Mrs. Brightman stood and readied herself to leave, George decided to do something he had never done before. He walked over to Mrs. Brightman and cleared his throat. "My dear woman," he began, "I can see you are trying hard to follow the ways of God, as we do. However, it's obvious you lack material provision and the money to buy yourself nourishing food. As my wife has told you, we often do not have much ourselves, but I would like to offer you whatever we have. We would like to share our money with you through a common purse. Whenever you need money, I want you to send a message to me, and I will share whatever we have with you. Now," he said reaching into his pocket, "let me give you enough to buy dinner on the train."

Mrs. Brightman spluttered and then burst into full laughter. Her whole body shook, and it was a good minute before she could regain her composure. "Whatever makes you think I need your money, Mr. Müller?" she finally asked.

George could feel his face turning red. "You said you didn't have money to buy dinner, and you have only one shawl," he said politely.

"No, no. I did not say I could not buy supper. I said I would not. I have a delicate stomach, and those greasy meals are not good for my digestion. As for my shawl, you are right, I have only one. But I can wear only one at a time, so it's sufficient for me, is it not?"

George nodded, not knowing what to say next. He had obviously insulted Mrs. Brightman by offering to share his money with her.

"I must go now," said Mrs. Brightman. "But before I do, let me tell you why I came here today. I recently inherited five hundred pounds, and I wanted to see if I should give it to the orphanage. So you see, I am not poor at all, Mr. Müller, and I certainly don't need your common purse."

When Mrs. Brightman was gone, George and Mary stood staring at each other.

"I had no idea," said Mary.

"Neither did I, but I certainly did insult her, didn't I? To think I offered to share our shilling or two with her when she had five hundred pounds in the bank!" groaned George.

The Müllers heard nothing more from Mrs. Brightman until one day several months later. George arrived home to find her once again sipping tea with Mary. She looked excited when George came in the door. "Mr. Müller," she began, "I thought much about what you said regarding sharing a common purse with me, and it touched me greatly. I know you do not have much, yet you were willing to share what little you had with me. I have decided to share what I have with you. A check for five hundred pounds will be arriving here within a month."

George and Mary had a special time of prayer that evening. Five hundred pounds would be enough to keep all three orphan houses running for at least a year.

By 1840, other people in England had become concerned about the plight of orphans and were addressing the problem in their own way. Charles Dickens published *Oliver Twist* that year. Through this famous author's book, upper-class English people were faced for the first time with the horrible reality of the lives of these children. The social tide was slowly beginning to turn in favor of protecting children from such awful circumstances. But there was still much to do.

While he was still busy with his various responsibilities, in the spring of 1843, George began thinking it was time to make another trip to Prussia. By this time, many people had written asking him to come. George was particularly impressed by a small group of Baptists who lived in Stuttgart. They were the first group of German Christians outside of the state-regulated church who had asked him for help, and he was eager to give it.

The more he thought about going, however, the more he knew he couldn't, at least not right away. There were too many obstacles. Before he would feel comfortable leaving Bristol, there needed to be at least two hundred pounds in the bank so the staff would not have to take on the responsibility of praying for the day-to-day operating expenses. Then there was the matter of the fourth orphan home on Wilson Street which was about to open. A suitable matron still had to be found to oversee the house. George had also decided that the next time he went home he would take Mary with him, and the total amount for their passage, plus money to live while they were away, was quite large. And lastly, George's book had been translated into German, but it had not yet been published because of the cost. If he went to Prussia, he wanted to be able to take copies of the German edition of his book to give away. The cost of publishing the German edition alone was two hundred pounds.

The amount of money George would need in hand before he could make the trip to Prussia quickly mounted up, especially for a man who was still praying for enough money to buy the next day's bread and milk for the orphans! Yet George and Mary had the faith to believe that God would provide the amount needed. They prayed and asked that if it was God's will for them to go to Prussia, He show it by providing the money they would need.

For almost a month after they began praying about the trip, the financial situation at the orphanages seemed to get worse. But George and Mary kept praying, and on July 12, 1843, they heard some wonderful news. A man whom George did not know gave him seven hundred pounds to be used for four purposes. First, some of the money was to be used among poor Christians in Bristol. Second, some of it was to be used to publish George's book in German. Three, some was to go towards running the orphan houses, and four, the balance was to be used to strengthen the faith of German Christians. In one day, George had the answer to all of his prayers, except a matron for the new orphan house at number four Wilson Street. She was hired a week later, leaving George and Mary feeling they could now travel to Prussia.

The Müllers stayed away six months, working among the churches in Stuttgart and distributing tracts and copies of George's book. Regrettably, Johann Müller, George's father, had died four years before, so Mary never had the opportunity to meet him.

In February 1844, the Müllers returned to Bristol and their work among the orphans.

Chapter 12

Do unto Others

George Müller peered at the address on the back of the envelope: 11 Wilson Street. As he opened the envelope, his pulse quickened. Maybe someone was offering him a fifth house on the street to rent! George hoped so. It was time to expand again, and houses on the street did not come up for rent very often. But as George read the letter, his heart sank. The letter was not about another house for rent at all. Quite the opposite. The writer, a resident of Wilson Street, wanted the orphans out of the neighborhood!

"Mary, Mary, come and read this," called George.

Mary arrived in the room with a pair of scissors still in her hand from cutting out aprons for the older girls to sew. "What is it, George?" she asked, catching her husband's worried look.

George handed her the letter, which she quickly read. "Oh, George, what are we going to do?" she groaned, as she sat down beside him.

"I don't know," replied George thoughtfully. "But he has a point, and if other residents on the street feel this way...." His voice tapered off as he reread the letter.

George had to admit that although the letter was not an unkind letter, it was blunt. The writer complained about the four orphan houses on Wilson Street. He laid out several areas of concern. One, the houses were very noisy, especially when the children were out playing in the corner lot. Two, the drains in the street backed up from overuse. Three, the water pressure was often reduced to a trickle because the orphan houses used so much water. The writer concluded by suggesting that George himself would not enjoy living next to his own orphan houses and asking George why the houses should be "inflicted" on the residents of Wilson Street.

"He has a point," said George, stroking his chin. "Each house was designed for no more than ten people to live in, and we have about thirty-five people in each of them. I think I would get a headache if I had to listen to the children playing for five or six hours a day."

Mary nodded. "But we can't make the orphanage disappear. I suppose you will have to meet with the man and see what you can do for him."

George sat silently. Jesus' admonition to do unto others as you would have them do unto you came to mind. George hadn't given it much thought before because no one had said anything, but he began to wonder whether he was being a good neighbor to the man who wrote the letter and the other residents of Wilson Street. Who really wanted to live next to so many rowdy children? But what could he do about it?

The more he thought about the situation, the more George felt he should move all the children out of Wilson Street. The letter writer had been correct. A group of orphan houses did not belong on a residential street. But if that was the case, where did they belong?

Over the next few hours, an idea began to take root in George's mind. What if he were to build an orphanage somewhere on the outskirts of town? He could make it large enough to house all the children under one roof. Such an idea for a man who often had to pray for a penny to buy a pint of milk was mind-boggling. Still, George had never been one to pass up an idea without praying about it first.

As he prayed, George felt that he should make a list of the good and bad points about building his own orphanage. He went to his desk and pulled out a sheet of crisp, white, writing paper. At the top he wrote, "Reasons for moving from Wilson Street." Under this heading he listed the reasons he thought it would be a good idea: (1) The neighbors have a just complaint about the orphan houses and the inconvenience they cause. (2) God is not honored when people feel they need to complain about having to live next to a Christian orphanage. (3) The playground on the corner was much too small for all of the children to play in at once. There was room for only one orphan house to use it at a time. (4) There were no grounds around the houses where the boys could plant gardens, both to teach the boys a useful skill and to provide some food for the homes. (5) The air in Bristol was smoky and polluted, and the children, many of whom arrived at the orphanage sick, would be healthier breathing country air. (6) When the children got sick, there was not enough room to separate them from the other children to ensure the illness did not spread.

Satisfied that he had listed all the reasons why it might be good to move the orphanage, George wrote a second heading, "Reasons for Remaining on Wilson Street," under which he listed the following reasons: (1) God has blessed us with first one, then two, three, and now four houses on Wilson Street. We would have to be very sure He was leading us to leave. (2) A lot of money would be required to move, money that could otherwise be used on the needs of the orphans. (3) It would take a tremendous amount of time to find the right site and plan and build a new orphanage.

For several hours George prayed over the two lists and finally came to the conclusion that it would be a good thing to build a new orphanage. More children than ever were on the waiting list, and having a larger facility that could accommodate them as well as the children already in the orphanages would make things a lot easier. The new facility would need only one huge kitchen, one laundry, and one heating system. Not only that, it would be wonderful to get the children out into the country a little. Since the children lived and went to school all within one block, they seldom got to experience nature.

Having settled it in his own mind, George decided to see whether other Christians could find any reason why he might be wrong in his thinking. At a regularly scheduled church prayer meeting that evening, he told the congregation about his idea. Everyone thought it was inspired. Once the building was paid for, a great deal of money would be saved in rent. As well, a permanent structure would be something the people of Bristol, both Christian and non-Christian, could point to as an example of what faith in God could do.

George and Mary began to pray in earnest for the project. They asked God to show them how they should proceed. George also gathered some important facts so that they could pray more specifically. It was good that they believed in a generous God, because if they didn't, the facts may well have discouraged them. They would need at least ten thousand pounds to construct a building large enough to house three hundred orphans!

With the facts in hand, the Müllers spent the next thirty-five mornings praying for a sign from God that they were supposed to begin building.

Each day nothing happened. But George did not get discouraged; he just kept praying and asking God to give him more faith to keep believing. Then on December 10, 1845, during their thirty-sixth morning of special prayer, they heard a knock on the door. A bank draft was delivered to the house, and with it a note saying the money was for building a new orphan house. The amount on the bank draft read, "one thousand pounds." It was the largest single donation George had ever received.

Three days later, Mary Müller's sister, who was living with George and Mary, returned to Bristol. She had been away in London, where she had met a man who had read George's book. She had introduced herself as George Müller's sister-in-law, and the two of them had struck up a conversation about the work that was going on in Bristol. In the course of the conversation, Mary's sister had mentioned the plan to build a new facility. The man's ears had pricked up, and the man announced he was an architect and would design and oversee the building of the new structure for free. He had apparently been praying for some way to serve God with his skills.

George was thoroughly excited. He already had a picture in his mind of how the new orphanage should look. The orphanage would be like no other building he had ever seen. It would not be built like other Victorian homes, but rather, every aspect of it would be thought out to serve the needs of the children as smoothly and efficiently as possible.

George now began to pray for the right site to build on. He knew they would need a large property—six or seven acres would be ideal—and the land would need to be on the outskirts of town. A building boom was going on in Bristol at that time, and the price of land was rising fast. Still, this did not concern George. As he had written in his journal, he believed that building an orphanage was God's idea, and therefore, as long as he did all he could, it was ultimately God's responsibility to make the dream a reality.

George and Mary continued with their morning prayer vigils, and on December 29, another fifty pounds was given towards the new orphanage. Then on January 3, one of the orphans stopped George as he was leaving number one Wilson Street. "Here, Mr. Müller," she said with shining eyes. "My aunt sent me some money for my birthday. I want you to have it for our new house." She handed George six pennies. He thanked her and returned home to record the gift in his account book. No amount was ever too small for George to record or be grateful for. The total donated so far for the new orphanage was now one thousand fifty pounds and sixpence.

The donation from the girl at the orphanage, small as it was, convinced George that it was time to start looking for a site for the new building. Later that morning, George prayed for God to guide him as he set off to look at a site that several people had suggested was suitable. But the more George walked around the site, which had been an armory, the more he knew it was not the right site for the new orphanage. It was in a slight hollow, which would make it extra damp in winter, and it did not catch the fresh westerly sea breeze.

As he walked home, George passed another piece of property, which, while it did not appear to be for sale, he felt drawn to. Was God telling him that this was the place to build the orphanage? George inquired at the next farmhouse as to who was the owner of the land. With the owner's name and address written on a piece of paper in his pocket, George went home to tell Mary what he had found.

"Is it for sale?" Mary asked him over dinner.

"When are the orphans moving?" asked thirteen-year-old Lydia. "I want to visit them all the time. It sounds so much fun to be out in the country. Promise I can spend some nights out there, please Papa?"

"Hold on," chuckled George. "There's a long way to go yet. I am going to write to the owner, but I'm not even sure if he will sell the land."

That night George wrote to the owner, and six days later he got a reply. The owner would sell the land, but for one thousand pounds an acre! While it sounded like a high price, it was actually quite reasonable. Yet George didn't feel he was to spend that much on land. He began to pray that God would either reduce the cost of the land or give him the patience to wait for an even better property.

A month had passed when a member of his congregation told George about another piece of property to the north of the city on Ashley Down. George and Lydia went to look at it. The property was only about a mile from Wilson Street, but the mile was straight up the side of a hill. Once George and Lydia reached the top of the hill, Ashley Down leveled off, and father and daughter enjoyed the breathtaking view of Bristol spread out below them.

"It's perfect, Papa," said Lydia "Look at the cows!"

Ashley Down was gentle and rolling and had large trees dotted across it. Cows grazed happily on the lush green grass, and a horse galloped back and forth in a pasture. The particular plot of land George had come to see was perfect for an orphanage, just as Lydia had observed. There were no neighbors, and the children would be free to make as much noise as they wanted. Not only that, the soil on Ashley Down would be good for the boys to plant their gardens in. And George could just imagine the view from the third-story windows, all the way to Stapleton in the east and Horfield to the north.

"Yes, Lydia," George told his daughter. "We must pray that God will show us if we are to have this property."

That evening, after George had finished answering his daily correspondence, he decided it was the right time to visit Mr. Hazelwood, the owner of the Ashley Down property. He walked to Mr. Hazelwood's home, only to be told that Mr. Hazelwood was still at work. George got the work address and strolled to the workplace, but when he arrived, the owner was not there either. So George decided to go home and try to contact Mr. Hazelwood the next day. On the way home, he prayed and asked God to cause the owner to accept a reasonable price for the land.

The next morning, February 5, 1846, George returned to Mr. Hazelwood's house. This time Mr. Hazelwood was in, and the butler invited George into the drawing room.

"Hello. Mr. Müller, I presume?" said a short, round man with a dark mustache a few moments later. The man strolled over and shook George's hand.

"Glad to meet you, Mr. Hazelwood," George said.

Mr. Hazelwood sat down in a brown leather chair opposite George. He looked as if he'd hardly slept the night before—his eyes were bloodshot and glazed. "Well, let's get down to business, shall we, Mr. Müller," he said. "As I understand from what my butler told me last night, you want to buy my property on Ashley Down for your orphans."

George nodded. "That's correct, sir."

Mr. Hazelwood leaned toward George and lowered his voice. "Well, let me tell you the strangest thing. Last night, when I heard you had been to visit, I decided to tell you the price was two hundred pounds an acre. A fair price by anyone's reckoning."

George nodded and waited for what Mr. Hazelwood would say next.

"Well, I went to bed, and about three this morning I woke up. No matter how hard I tried I couldn't get back to sleep. Nor could I escape the feeling as I lay awake that I was to offer you the land for one hundred and twenty pounds per acre. By breakfast time, I was convinced that's what I should do. I won't make the profit I intended to on the property, but I hope I will get a better night's sleep tonight!"

George was delighted. He was certain this was God's answer to his prayer for land on which to build the new orphanage. A deal to buy the land was quickly struck, and right there and then all the paperwork was filled out. By evening, George Müller was the owner of seven acres of beautiful land on Ashley Down. And he had paid a total of eight hundred forty pounds for it, less than the price of a single acre of the other property. At once he wrote to the architect in London, asking him whether he was still interested in helping to design and supervise the building of the orphanage.

Chapter 13

Ashley Down

On the morning of February 12, 1849, a visitor handed George two thousand pounds to complete the huge square brick orphanage on Ashley Down. With the donation, George estimated that after all the expenses were paid, there would probably be several hundred pounds left over. He noted in his journal, "The Lord not only gives as much as is absolutely necessary for His work, but He gives abundantly."

It had been a difficult three years since the purchase of the property on Ashley Down. The whole of England had fallen into economic turmoil. Bread and rice had doubled in price, oatmeal had tripled, and potatoes had become so expensive they disappeared from the menu altogether. More children than ever were in need of help, especially Irish children whose parents had crossed the Irish Sea to England to flee the potato famine. If the parents died in England, often there was not a single relative or friend to care for the orphans, many of whom were sent to George Müller's orphanage.

As George oversaw the completion of the new orphanage on Ashley Down, he was glad it was large enough to house three hundred children. Not only would it comfortably hold the one hundred twenty children currently in the Wilson Street orphan homes, but also it would allow George to take in the many other orphan children who came to him for help.

Finally, Monday, June 18, 1849, arrived. It was a day that many in Bristol would not soon forget. The children marched in two orderly lines from Wilson Street up Ashley Down hill to their new home. George and Mary were there to greet them when they arrived and listen to their gasps of delight as they ran their hands over the smooth, beautifully polished banisters and peeked into the well-equipped kitchen.

"Is this all for us?" asked one little boy, his eyes wide with wonder.

"It's ever so grand," responded one of the newest orphan girls.

George smiled at her. "Everything you see here is a reflection of God's love for you," he said. "Now run along and find out where your bedroom is."

People had said George was crazy, that he should be content with helping a few children, that there was a limit to how much money people, even Christian people, would be willing to give to the orphanage. And while George agreed with them, he smiled to himself. There were limits to how much people would give, but, as long as he obeyed God, there were no limits to the amount of money God could provide to take care of the orphans.

Of course, moving one family is a large and complicated task, but moving one hundred twenty children, twenty adults, and the furniture and belongings from four houses took some planning and four full days of labor to complete. The first orphanage at number six Wilson Street had been open for thirteen years, and in that time, it had managed to collect a wide variety of items.

At the new orphanage everything was unpacked in an orderly manner. The house was divided into large rooms for the various age groupings of children. The babies and toddlers were housed in a room with a row of small cribs along one side. On the other side of the room were a number of cubbyholes filled with toys for the children to play with. The southern end of the room was set up as a diaper-changing area. With up to sixty children in diapers at any one time, the laundry was kept very busy!

The older children's rooms were set up with places to practice the practical skills they learned in school. All of the older children, both boys and girls, were taught to knit, and they made all of the stockings and the socks for the orphanage. The older children were also taught to mend their own clothes and darn their own socks.

George accepted between five and eight new orphans a week. Because many of the children came from dreadful conditions, they brought with them a constant threat of deadly diseases like typhoid and cholera. Special care was taken to ensure that everything was kept clean. The children each had a little bag with their toiletries in it, and the bags hung in neat rows in the bathroom.

Every Wednesday afternoon visitors were welcomed and shown through the orphan house and surrounding gardens and playgrounds. Visitors were impressed with the orderliness of everything and with the happy, well cared for children. On some occasions, the visitors were well-known or famous. Not long after the new orphanage opened on Ashley Down, Charles Dickens arrived unannounced. The author explained to George that he had heard some horrible rumors about the place and had come to investigate. These rumors suggested that the children were treated like slaves, that there was not enough food for them to eat, and that the rooms were rat infested. George had heard them all before. And while they frustrated and disappointed him, he dismissed them by telling himself that when a person tried to do something different, there were those who attempted to spoil it any way they could. When he learned that Charles Dickens had heard these rumors, he called one of his assistants and gave him a set of keys. "Take Mr. Dickens anywhere on the property he desires to go," he instructed the assistant. "Open any door he asks to see behind, and do not bring him back until he is completely satisfied he's seen everything he wants to."

"Where would you like to start, Mr. Dickens?" asked the assistant.

The two men walked out of George's office and did not return for three hours. And when they did, Charles Dickens was full of praise for all he had seen. He promised to write an article squelching the rumors once and for all.

George was pleased with the way things were progressing, except for one thing. News of the opening of the new orphanage had been reported in many newspapers around the British Isles. These reports heralded the orphanage as a bold new experiment where any orphan child who applied was given a safe and comfortable place to live, grow, and attend school. Although this reporting had some positive effects (people learned how the orphanage was funded, and some, like one of Queen Victoria's chaplains, sent money to support the work), it also had a downside. People from all over the British Isles began to send orphan children. It was not unusual for a child to walk up to the orphanage on Ashley Down with nothing more than a note that read, "To the orphan man in Bristol" or "The free orphanage." And of course, George took the children in. What else could he do when the only alternative was to send them to the poorhouse? But before the orphanage was a year old, it was filled to capacity with three hundred orphans. Soon it had a waiting list with over one hundred children's names on it. Once again, George Müller felt something more had to be done.

George started off 1851 by praying and asking God to show him the next step to take. Within a few days, he received a donation of three thousand pounds, the single largest donation he had so far received. George took the money as a sign he should expand the orphanage. He estimated it would cost about thirty-five thousand pounds to build a new building to accommodate seven hundred more orphans. As before, he got busy praying and asking God to provide the money he needed. Many people might have felt burdened having to believe God for such a large sum of money, but not George Müller. George wrote in his journal, "The greatness of the sum required affords me a kind of secret joy; for the greater the difficulty to be overcome, the more will it be seen to the glory of God how much can be done by prayer and faith."

As had happened before, the orphans themselves gave the little money they had, and George recorded their halfpennies and pennies in his ledger along with the large donations.

At the same time that George was trusting God for money to construct another building, the orphanage suffered through times of financial stress. There were times when there wasn't a shilling left to run the place. But every time George prayed, just enough money would arrive to meet the daily operating costs. As in times like these before, George would not take money that had been given for one purpose and use it on another, no matter how desperate the need. Not one pound of the three thousand pounds given for the new building was ever used for the day-to-day expenses of the orphanage. George kept track of every penny. Not a single coin went somewhere the giver had not intended for it to go.

Sometimes, people on the other side of the world who had heard about the orphanage or read George's book sent money. A little girl who lived on a farm in New Zealand sent George a shilling that she had earned by selling hens' eggs. A shepherd in Australia sent a banknote after someone had given him a copy of George's book to read while herding his sheep. Some people did not give money but instead gave valuable items. It was quite common for a package to arrive at the orphanage filled with rings, pearl necklaces, and broaches to be sold and the money used for the orphanage. George often smiled to himself when he received these packages. It reminded him of the time after he and Mary were first married and he had asked her to sell her family's silverware. Now it appeared that many other people were giving up or selling their possessions for the orphans. Someone even donated three autographs from the late king, William IV, one from Sir Robert Peel, and two from Lord Melbourne. Someone else donated a rare antique Coverdale English Bible. One of the secretaries at the orphanage had the job of selling these items, some of which fetched a substantial amount of money.

On May 29, 1855, ground was broken for the second orphan house. George's plan for a single building to house seven hundred orphans had been changed to two buildings, one to house three hundred orphans and the other, four hundred. This change had been made so that the buildings could fit better on the existing property. The buildings would flank the existing structure, which was now known as "Number One Orphan House."

In November 1857, Number Two Orphan House was opened, with space for two hundred infant girls and two hundred girls aged eight and over. Number Three Orphan House remained in the planning stage.

With the increase in the size of the orphanage, there was, of course, an enormous amount of work for George to do every day. Some decisions, such as adding a path from the outdoor playing pavilion directly to Number Two Orphan House, were easy to make. Others were more complicated, such as the time Eric, the maintenance man, came to George's office.

"It's the boiler in Number One," Eric told George, taking off his grubby hat and pushing his hair out of his eyes.

"What's the problem?" asked George, motioning for Eric to sit down and warm himself beside the radiator.

"It's leaking, plain and simple, sir, and serious, too. The most serious I've ever seen. It shouldn't be doing that—it's only eight years old."

"What do you think is causing the leak?" asked George.

"That I can't say. We'd need to get inside the boiler to find that out."

George thought for a moment. "That would mean taking all the fire bricks out of the boiler, wouldn't it?" he inquired.

Eric nodded. "And that's the catch, sir. It's going to take at least two days to take them out, find the leak, seal it, and reline the boiler with the bricks. Then of course, we mightn't even be able to fix it, and we'll have to get a new boiler. Now that would be a big job. Could take a fortnight or longer...."

"Yes," said George, interrupting him and thinking of how the boiling water from the boiler fed the radiators for the whole of Number One Orphan House. "No matter what happens, the children must not go cold. I'll let you know what we'll do about it as soon as I can, Eric."

Eric nodded, put his cap back on, and respectfully left the office.

George knew he had a difficult decision to make. It was nearly December, and it often began to snow around this time of year. If the boiler was shut down for several days, the house would become unbearably cold—too cold for young orphan children to stay in without catching colds or the flu. On the other hand, if he did nothing, the boiler could break down, cutting off the supply of hot water for even longer. George did the only thing he knew to do; he prayed about it.

Over the next day or so, he prayed one, that the wind would shift to the south so that it brought warmer weather, and two, that God would give workmen a "mind to work" so that the boilers would not need to be turned off any longer than was absolutely necessary.

Convinced that this was the right course of action, George made arrangements for some tradesmen to come on the morning of December 9, 1857, to repair the boiler. For a week leading up to this date, a frigid north wind had blown steadily and had shown no sign of letting up. On the night of December 8, the wind howled across Ashley Down and whistled around the window panes of Number One Orphan House.

"It's a miracle, Mr. Müller, a miracle," said Eric as he greeted George the next morning. "The wind has turned to the south, and the weather is positively balmy."

Indeed, during the night, the wind had shifted one hundred eighty degrees and was now blowing warm air out of the south.

"We stopped stoking the boiler at midnight, and it's been right mild ever since. If this keeps up, we won't need any heat at all," continued Eric.

George smiled. It was exactly what he had prayed for.

In the basement beside the boiler the tradesmen were gathered waiting for permission to begin their task. George thanked them all for coming, he said a prayer, and the men set to work. They worked hard all day, and when evening came and George went to check on their progress, the foreman offered to have the men work late into the evening and then come back first thing in the morning to finish the job.

"But sir," interrupted one of the boilermakers. "If you don't mind, the rest of us have discussed it, and we would rather stay and work all night until we finish the job."

George watched the foreman's eyebrows raise in surprise.

"It's for the orphans, a special case, you know," added the boilermaker.

"If that's what you want to do, it's fine with me," said the foreman. "But you still have a full day's work ahead of you tomorrow. Don't think I'm going to let you go home and sleep."

"We understand," said the boilermaker with a shrug. "It's just something we want to do, that's all."

George left the basement with a smile on his face. Indeed, these men had a "mind to work!"

By the time George Müller arrived at Ashley Down the following morning, the leak had been repaired, and the boiler was in the process of being relined with fire bricks. That part of the job was finished late in the afternoon, and soon after, boiling water was once again coursing through the radiators. And during the time the boiler was out of action, not one child was even chilled.

Once again, George Müller thanked God for watching over the orphans in his care. And once again a plan was taking root in his mind, a plan to get construction of Number Three Orphan House under way. However, the house would now accommodate four hundred fifty more children, not the three hundred originally planned for it. The work with the orphans continued to grow and grow.

Chapter 14

God Will Supply

By 1862, George Müller had two assistants. Jim Wright helped run the Scriptural Knowledge Institution for Home and Abroad, and John Townsend helped George with his church work, especially running the Sunday schools. John Townsend became a particularly close friend to George, as did his wife Caroline and daughter Abigail. Abigail was three years old when her parents moved to Bristol, and she came to look upon George and Mary almost as grandparents.

Early one morning, when she was eight years old, Abigail came to visit the orphanage. In his office, George was busy discussing with Jim Wright how many new tracts the Scripture Knowledge Institution should print. When he looked up from the discussion, through his office window he could see Abigail playing happily in the garden. George smiled to himself. He was still smiling and looking out the window when there was a knock at the door. A moment later the matron of Number One Orphan House walked in.

"I hate to bother you, Mr. Müller," began the matron, "but it's happened. The children are all ready for breakfast and there is not a thing in the house to eat. What shall I tell them?"

George stood up. "I'll take care of it. Just give me a minute," he said.

Before going to the dining room at Number One Orphan House, George walked out into the garden. "Abigail, Abigail, come here," he called.

Abigail ran up to him. "What is it?" she asked.

George reached down and took her hand. "Come and see what God will do," he said as he escorted her to the dining room.

Inside they found three hundred children standing in neat rows behind their chairs. Set on the table in front of each child were a plate, a mug, and a knife, fork, and spoon. But there was no food whatsoever to be seen. George watched as Abigail's eyes grew wide with astonishment. "But, where's the food?" Abigail asked in a whisper.

"God will supply," George told her quietly, before he turned to address the children. "There's not much time. I don't want any of you to be late for school, so let us pray," he announced.

As the children bowed their heads, George simply prayed, "Dear God, we thank you for what you are going to give us to eat. Amen."

George looked up and smiled at the children. "You may be seated," he said. He had no idea at all where the food he had just prayed for would come from or how it would get to the orphanage. He just knew God would not fail the children.

A thunderous din filled the room as three hundred chairs were scuffed across the wooden floor. Soon all three hundred children sat obediently in front of their empty plates.

No sooner had the noise in the dining room subsided than there was a knock at the door. George walked over and opened the door. In the doorway stood the baker, holding a huge tray of delicious-smelling bread.

"Mr. Müller," began the baker, "I couldn't sleep last night. I kept thinking that somehow you would need bread this morning and that I was supposed to get up and bake it for you. So I got up at two o'clock and made three batches for you. I hope you can use it."

George smiled broadly. "God has blessed us through you this morning," he said as he took the tray of bread from the baker.

"There's two more trays out in the cart," said the baker. "I'll fetch them."

Within minutes, the children were all eating freshly baked bread. As they were enjoying it, there was a second knock at the door. This time it was the milkman, who took off his hat and addressed George. "I'm needing a little help, if you could, sir. The wheel on my cart has broken, right outside your establishment. I'll have to lighten my load before I can fix it. There's ten full cans of milk on it. Could you use them?" Then looking at the orphans, sitting in neat rows, he added, "Free of charge, of course. Just send someone out to get them. I'll never fix the cart with all that weight on it."

George dispatched twenty of the older children to help, and soon they had the ten cans of milk stowed in the kitchen, where it was dispensed with a ladle. There was enough milk for every child to have a mug full and enough left over for them all to have some in their tea at lunch.

Half an hour after George and Abigail had entered the dining room, three hundred orphans with full stomaches filed out.

George escorted Abigail back to the garden, where he watched her sit for a long time. He knew she was thinking about what she had just seen. Several weeks later, Caroline Townsend told George that Abigail had taken to finishing all her prayer requests with, "like you do for George Müller. Amen." This made George happy. It was exactly the point he had wanted Abigail to see. God does answer prayer.

The visitors kept coming to see the Ashley Down orphanage. Many were impressed with what George Müller had achieved through prayer. One of these visitors was thirty-three-year-old Hudson Taylor, with his wife Maria and the first sixteen missionary recruits for the newly formed China Inland Mission. The group spent most of the day, August 22, 1865, visiting with George and Mary. George and Hudson Taylor walked and talked together in the garden for a long time. Before the group left, George promised to pray regularly for them as they set sail for China. In some ways, George wished he could go with them. Over the years, the challenge of foreign ports and millions of people who had not yet heard the gospel message had lost none of its lure for him. But he knew that God had given him a mission field among the orphans of Bristol, many of whom had never heard of God or salvation through His Son Jesus. And besides, George told himself, he was getting too old to start in on a new missionary adventure.

While George loved to work hard, occasionally he was able to be persuaded to take a break. During these times, the Müller family would spend several days at the seaside town of Ilfracombe, west of Bristol, where George loved to walk around the harbor and climb the surrounding hills.

In the autumn of 1865, George, Mary, and Lydia went to Ilfracombe for a few days' rest. September 4 dawned a beautiful, clear day. The three of them set out to trek to the top of Capstone Hill. From the summit they enjoyed a panoramic view of the surrounding area. On their way down from the summit, they met a group of people going the other way. A tall blond man in the group tipped his hat as he passed them and then turned around to follow them. "Excuse me," he called, "aren't you George Müller?

"Yes," replied George, surprised that anyone would recognize him in such an unusual setting.

"I have money that I need to give you for the orphans," the man said.

The two men sat down on a nearby bench to talk for a few minutes. George learned that the man was a businessman from the nearby town of Minehead. The man had read several of the annual reports from the orphanage and was amazed that so many children were fed and clothed through prayer alone.

"Anyway," said the businessman, looking directly at George. "At first I doubted your approach, so I decided to put it to the test. There was a piece of property I wanted to buy, and I had it valued. I then found out it was going to be sold at auction, so I put in a ridiculously low bid on it ahead of time and prayed and promised God that if I got the land I would give you one hundred pounds. By the time the auction came, I was so anxious to know what had happened that I caught the train out to where the land was being auctioned. To my amazement I found my bid had been accepted. I am now the owner of a valuable piece of property, and I purchased it for only a quarter of what it's worth. I went to Bristol to give you the one hundred pounds, but I was told you were here in Ilfracombe, so I came to find you. I will bring the money to you if you tell me where you are staying."

George smiled. "Thank you," he said. "I am not surprised God blessed you with the land. I have heard many similar stories over the years, though I must confess it is amazing to me how people in so many parts of the country come to hear about the work of the orphanage. Now, you said you were from Minehead?"

"Yes," replied the man.

"I cannot remember anyone from Minehead ever giving to the orphanage, but strangely, within the space of a week, two people from there want to give me money. Before I left Bristol, I received word from a lawyer in Minehead that a man wants to leave the orphanage a legacy of one thousand pounds in his will. The lawyer did not give the man's name, but I find it quite remarkable, since I am not acquainted with a single person from there."

A broad smile lit the businessman's face. "Since you mentioned it, I will confess. I am the man who has left you the legacy! When I realized I had been wrong to doubt the power of prayer, I decided to make a will and leave you one thousand pounds to help carry on the orphan work."

"So you have learned the power of prayer and of giving all in one lesson!" said George, with a beaming smile. "Showing Christians that God is able to answer prayer was one of the reasons I decided to build the orphanage at Ashley Down."

The two men talked on for several more minutes before they went their separate ways. Later than afternoon, George received the one hundred pounds.

The following January, George's friend and associate Henry Craik died from heart problems at the age of sixty, the same age as George. The funeral was held at Bethesda Chapel. It was a solemn day for George as he climbed into the pulpit to conduct the funeral service for his old friend and trusted adviser. The two men had been friends for thirty-six years.

After Henry Craik's death, many people who worked with George began to worry about him and Mary. How long could they survive the hectic pace they set themselves? How many other sixty-year-old men hand wrote over three thousand letters a year, preached three times a week, and oversaw the work of three separate ministries? And how many sixty-eight-year-old women inspected every shipment of supplies that came into an orphanage or personally arranged for the sewing and mending of over ten thousand complete outfits of clothing, not to mention regularly going over all the accounts to make sure they were kept accurately? The pace, however, did not slow down the Müllers one bit. Orphans were still being sent to the poorhouses or living on the streets in Great Britain, and George would not rest until he had done all he could to help them.

Four months later, in May 1866, ground was broken for Number Four Orphan House. The house was completed in November of the following year, and work on Number Five Orphan House was immediately begun. On January 6, 1870, the last of the orphan houses was completed, and the children moved in. Now, in the five orphan houses, George Müller and his workers were caring for two thousand fifty children!

Every child who came to the orphanage had his or her own story of how he or she came to be there. One of the stories that was recorded concerned William Ready, who was born in a London poorhouse early in 1860. William's mother died soon after William was born, leaving him and his nine brothers and sisters in the care of their drunkard father, who died in 1865. The ten children had become orphans.

When their father died, William Ready and his brothers and sisters begged to be allowed to leave the poorhouse. They made up a story about a relative who was waiting for them. In truth, they had nowhere to go, but they wanted to get away from the terrible conditions in the poorhouse. The children lived on the streets, scavenging whatever they could find to eat, an orange peel here, an apple core there, a rotten banana from the garbage. Anything that could stave off their gnawing hunger pangs was quickly scooped up and gulped down with delight. Sometimes William even collected and ate cigar butts so there would at least be something in his stomach. On the weekends, William and his older brothers went to pubs, where they sang funny songs and did acrobatics for a penny or two.

All in all, it was a grim life, and one from which very few children ever grew to be adults. William

Ready, though, survived in spite of the odds. A Christian man from St. George's Church in Bloomsbury noticed William when he was twelve years old. He asked William if he would like to live in an orphanage. William eagerly said yes, not because he knew what an orphanage was but because anything sounded better than the life he was leading.

A week later, William Ready was not a happy boy. He had been taken to the orphanage at Ashley Down, where he was scrubbed from head to toe, given a haircut, and told to wear a uniform of brown corduroy trousers, white shirt, button-up vest, and navy blue Eton coat. He told the matron he felt like a stuffed chicken. Worse still, he had to go to school each day. It didn't take the teacher long to figure out that William could not read or write a single word. So at twelve years of age, William had to begin his studies with the kindergarten children.

Finally, William settled into the routine, and after several years, he was one of the top students in the school. Mr. French, the person at the orphanage in charge of finding employment for the boys, asked William if he would like to become a flour miller. William thought that would be a fine occupation. Soon, his final day at the orphanage approached. As with all the children who left the orphanage, William was given three new sets of clothes to take with him. The orphanage also paid his apprenticeship fee, which amounted to his first year's wages.

The last thing each child did before leaving the orphanage was to have a final interview with George

Müller. George looked up from his desk when he heard the knock at the door. "Come in," he said.

William Ready walked in, and George motioned for him to sit down.

"Well, lad, it's time for you to leave us," George said fondly.

"Yes, sir," replied William respectfully.

George opened a draw in his desk, pulled out a half-crown (a coin worth two shillings and six-pence), and walked over to where William Ready was sitting. "Hold out your hands, lad," he said, picking up a Bible from the table beside him.

When William held out his hands, George placed the Bible in his right hand and the coin in his left. "You can hold on more tightly to something in your right hand than you can to something in your left hand, can you not?" he asked.

William Ready nodded.

"Well, wherever you go, remember this. If you hold tightly to the teaching in the Bible, God will always give you something in your other hand to hold as well."

After George had prayed for William, he shook his hand and wished him the best in his life ahead.

Like so many of the other orphans, William Ready kept in touch with George by letter, and he sent money whenever he could to help raise other orphan children—children unknown to either of them that day in George's office. George and William were destined to meet again, though, many years later and thousands of miles from Bristol.

Chapter 15

Traveling Days

"My dear, you don't look well," said George with great concern. "Why don't you go back to bed and let me send for Dr. Pritchard."

"No, really, I mean...," Mary Müller's voice trailed off as she leaned on the dressing table to keep her balance. "I do feel a bit dizzy. I might go back to bed, if you think you could possibly do without me for today."

Mary folded the covers back and climbed into bed. "I know there is still so much to do. After all, Number Five Orphan House has been open only a week. I wanted to finish sewing the drapes for the dining room windows, and I wonder if you could visit Johnny Smalley—he was looking pale yesterday. I hope he isn't coming down with something serious."

"Just rest, and let me take care of things," said George, patting Mary's hand. "I will send for the doctor."

George was very worried. In the twenty-one years the orphanage on Ashley Down had been open, Mary had never spent a day in bed sick. Something serious was wrong with his wife; he could feel it.

An hour later, Dr. Pritchard was standing in the hallway talking to George and Lydia. "I'm afraid to tell you, but Mrs. Müller is a very sick woman. She has rheumatic fever. I've given her some medicine to keep her comfortable, but there's not much else I can do. I'm sorry."

George spent much of the rest of the day with his ailing wife, praying for her and talking over the affairs of the orphanage. He wished he could spend the whole day at her side, but there were some important things at the orphanage only he could take care of. As he got up to leave the room, he said softly, "My darling, I'm sorry to leave you, but I will return as soon as I can."

Mary turned to her husband and with joy on her face replied, "You leave me with Jesus."

The next day, Sunday, February 6, 1870, Mary Müller died, leaving George, Lydia, and two thousand orphans to mourn her.

Five days later, George conducted her funeral service at Bethesda Chapel. He spoke of her love for the orphans and the hard work she had done on their behalf for thirty-four years. He preached a short message at the funeral based on Psalm 119:68: "Thou art good, and doest good." There was hardly a dry eye among the congregation by the time he had finished speaking of his gratitude to God for giving him such a wonderful wife for thirty-nine years and four months.

The funeral service was one of the largest Bristol had ever seen. Thousands of people who could not squeeze into the chapel waited silently outside, ready to walk beside the coffin to the cemetery.

After the funeral, hundreds of letters poured in from adults who had lived in the orphanage as children. Many of the writers expressed their love for Mary and shared their memories of Wilson Street and Ashley Down. One woman wrote, "I was only a small child then, and am still a child when I think of Ashley Down. It was a lovely, lovely spot...and no place ever seemed so dear."

Another wrote, "True, I never knew my parents, to know what it was to love them; but I do know what it is to love you and her [Mary Müller] and from my heart I mourn her loss. I know you miss her daily."

George was comforted by these letters and the many others like them, but he could not help but miss Mary in a thousand little ways each day. He missed their times of prayer together in the morning, the way she visited the sick children each day and gave him a report on their condition, the delight she felt over showing the older girls a new embroidery stitch or rocking a baby until it fell asleep. The orphan houses were not the same without Mary. Before long, George came to the conclusion that it would be better to have them run by a married couple rather than a sixty-five-year-old widower.

George and Mary had often prayed about who should replace them and run the orphanage, and long ago they had agreed that it should be Jim Wright. The Müllers had known Jim for twenty-five years, since he was a teenager. For the past twelve years, Jim had been George's assistant, running the Scriptural Knowledge Institution for Home and Abroad, where he had proved himself to be hard-working, kind, and faithful.

With Mary gone, George felt it was time to ask Jim Wright to consider becoming his successor and start taking over some of the responsibility for running the orphanage. At first, Jim refused to even think about it. Over several months, though, he and his wife Annie agreed that Jim should begin to step into the role. No sooner had they made the decision than Annie died after a sudden illness, leaving *two* widowers in charge of the orphanage! Thankfully, Lydia Müller took on many of her mother's responsibilities, and together she, George, and Jim Wright kept everything running smoothly. As they all worked together, something wonderful happened—Jim and Lydia fell in love.

Eighteen months after his wife died, Jim Wright married Lydia Müller at Bethesda Chapel. Lydia was thirty-nine years old, and Jim was forty-five.

It was a joyous day, though Lydia carried a tiny shadow of guilt about leaving her father alone in the family home on Paul Street.

Lydia need not have worried. When George saw how happy Lydia and Jim were, he decided to remarry himself. He had known Susannah Sangar for more than twenty-five years, from the time she had begun attending Bethesda Chapel as a twenty-year-old. Now, Susannah was in her midforties, and George came to believe she would make a wonderful wife for him and partner in his work. Susannah was as direct as Mary had been and was a very hard worker. When George asked her to marry him, she eagerly agreed. The two of them were married on November 30, 1871, two weeks after Lydia's wedding!

Susannah Müller was twenty-one years younger than her new husband and was brimming with energy. Suddenly George found he had a lot of things to look forward to. Since Jim and Lydia were more than capable of running the orphanage, George felt it was time to give his attention more fully to other projects. He was well-known as a wonderful preacher around the south of England, and he had been begged time after time to speak at some of the largest Christian gatherings of the day. In the spring of 1875, George and Susannah began a short preaching tour around England.

Although George was seventy, he had never felt healthier. He preached for Charles Spurgeon at the famous Metropolitan Tabernacle; he preached at outdoor meetings, in Brethren chapels, and in other churches around the country. Everywhere he went, people wanted to know whether it was really true that he supported two thousand orphans and never asked for a penny from anyone but God. George loved to tell them the stories of miraculous provision and assure them that God does indeed answer prayer.

The tour was such a success that the Müllers went on a second one, this time traveling all the way to Scotland. When they returned to Bristol, Lydia fussed around her father, worried that he might have overtaxed himself. But the opposite was true. George had come back invigorated and ready for more. His next preaching trip took him to other parts of Europe, where for the first time in thirty-one years he got to preach in his native German.

Wherever George preached, enormous crowds gathered. In Bern, Switzerland, two thousand people came to hear him. Many members of European royalty also came, including several of Queen Victoria's daughters who had married European princes. Since he could speak six languages fluently, George rarely needed a translator when he preached.

In the spring of 1877, George Müller found himself back at Halle University, where he had arrived as a student fifty-two years before. He was invited to preach at Franke's Orphanage, where he had stayed for a time. As he showed his wife around the town, George was flooded with memories. He thought about the time he had wasted in the ale houses, the first Christian meeting he attended, and Dr. Tholuck, who had first suggested he apply to go to England to learn how to communicate with Jews.

On their way back to England, George and Susannah traveled to Holland to meet a man with whom George had corresponded for many years. This Dutch man had been so inspired by George's example that he'd started his own orphanage in Nimegen. It gave George great pleasure to speak to the four hundred fifty Dutch orphans who were being cared for as a result of his inspiration. By the time he returned to England, George had preached over three hundred times.

When George arrived home, he found a letter waiting for him inviting him to come and preach in North America. George knew he needed to rest a while, but he could think of nothing that he would rather do than encourage American Christians. While he rested, Susannah, in her usual efficient way, arranged an itinerary for him. On August 23, 1877, the couple boarded the *Sardinian,* bound for Quebec, Canada, where George was to begin his speaking tour.

George took every opportunity during the ocean voyage to hand out Bible literature and speak to the crew about the gospel message. It was not until the ship was off the coast of Newfoundland, though, that his words made any impression on the captain.

A thick fog had engulfed the ship, forcing it to slow to a crawl for fear of being wrecked along the rocky coastline. As a result, the ship began to fall behind in its schedule. Concerned that he would not make his first speaking engagement, George headed for the bridge in search of the captain.

"So there you are," George said when he found the captain huddled over a map on the bridge. "I must tell you that I need to be in Quebec by Saturday afternoon."

The captain laughed out loud. "Why, that's impossible, Mr. Müller. Whoever is waiting for you will just have to understand this ship is fog bound, and there's not a thing I can do about it."

"In that case," said George matter-of-factly, "if you cannot find a way to get me there on time, I'll have to ask God to do it. I have not missed a single engagement in fifty-two years, and I don't intend to start now. Come down to my cabin with me, and we will pray together."

The captain looked too surprised to speak. George left the bridge, and the captain followed him meekly. As they walked onto deck, the captain came to his senses and protested. "But what's the point of praying? The fog is so thick I cannot see to the stern." He leaned over the rail. "Take a look for yourself, Mr. Müller."

"I don't need to look," replied George, walking purposefully towards the stairwell. "My eye is not on the weather, but on the One who controls the weather!"

George strolled into his cabin and shut the door firmly behind them both.

"Let us pray," he said, kneeling beside his bunk. The captain followed his example and got awkwardly down on his knees.

"Dear God," began George, "I come to You now to ask You to do the impossible. You know that I need to be in Quebec by Saturday and that the fog has hemmed us in. Please lift the fog so that the ship can go forward and I will be on time. Amen."

George opened his eyes and turned to look at the captain.

"Dear God," began the captain in a shaky, embarrassed voice.

George placed his hand on the captain's shoulder. "There's no need for you to pray. You don't believe God will answer prayer, and I believe He already has," he said.

With a grateful expression on his face, the captain clambered to his feet.

"Go and open the door," instructed George with an air of certainty. "I have known my Lord for fifty-two years, and in all that time I cannot recall a single instance where he has not answered my prayers. I can assure you, the fog has lifted."

The captain walked to the cabin door and opened it carefully. He peered out onto the deck and then turned back to George, his face pale with shock. "It's gone," he said, his voice barely above a whisper. "Just like you prayed, the fog has gone."

And so it had. There was not a trace of it. The next day the *Sardinian* docked in Quebec, but not before the captain had become a Christian convert. George disembarked and had plenty of time to reach his first preaching appointment on time.

From Quebec, George and Susannah made their way down the coast into the United States. George preached about fifty times in the New York area. In Chicago he preached in Moody's Tabernacle, where seven thousand people gathered to hear him. Along the way, he hardly entered a city without meeting one of his orphans who had emigrated to the United States.

On January 10, 1878, at 9:30 in the morning, George and Susannah Müller had an appointment no one would want to pass up. They had been invited to the White House to meet with President and Mrs. Hayes. They stayed for nearly an hour, during which time the president asked many questions about their work in Bristol.

George and Susannah continued their journey by rail and riverboat, going as far south as Georgia and then all the way to the Pacific Ocean to San Francisco. They stayed in California for a month before making their way slowly back to the East Coast. On June 27, by the time they boarded the *Adriatic* for Liverpool, they had traveled nearly twenty thousand miles and George had preached over three hundred times.

His next speaking tour took George once again to other parts of Europe. Then, in 1879, because so many American Christians had written begging George to return, the Müllers set out for the United

States once more. George was now seventy-four years old, but he felt better than he had when he was half that age.

In 1881, George and Susannah set out on a speaking trip that included Egypt, Palestine, Turkey, and Greece. They visited the pyramids and climbed the Mount of Olives in Jerusalem, and George preached at the Wailing Wall. Everywhere they went, they shared the gospel message and handed out New Testaments in many languages.

Over the next several years, the Müllers' tours covered China, Hong Kong, India, Rome (Italy), Australia, and New Zealand. In New Zealand, George visited and stayed with William Ready, the London orphan boy for whom he had arranged to become an apprentice flour miller. William had emigrated to New Zealand, where he was now one of the country's best-loved ministers.

At one point, the Müllers found themselves riding in a crowded train on their way to the city of Dunedin in the South Island of New Zealand. The man in the seat opposite them was totally absorbed in the newspaper he was reading. From time to time, he would read an article aloud to entertain or inform the other passengers.

As the train rumbled along through the rolling New Zealand countryside, the man began to read aloud. "The Reverend George Müller is about to grace the city of Dunedin with a visit. The Reverend and Mrs. Müller have been on an extensive tour of New Zealand, sharing their faith and their belief that God listens to and answers the prayers of his children. Indeed it appears to be true, since…." The man stopped reading in midsentence and looked up from the newspaper. With great conviction he said, "I would give almost anything to see him."

"You are looking right at him. I am George Müller," said George quietly, much to the man's astonishment.

George spent the rest of the journey answering passengers' questions and inviting people to come and hear him speak at Garrison Hall in Dunedin.

The Müllers were in India in January 1890 when they received sad news via telegram from their son-in-law Jim Wright. George's daughter Lydia had died unexpectedly at the age of fifty-seven. George and Susannah made their way to Bombay to await passage back to England. Even in his distress, George Müller never passed up an opportunity to preach and tell people about God. While they waited for their ship to depart for England, George preached fifteen times in a large tent that had been set up on the waterfront. He also preached once in German to the crew of a German man-of-war ship docked in the harbor. As soon and as quickly as they could, George and Susannah made their way back to Bristol to console Jim Wright and help him carry on the work with the orphans.

The Müllers went on two more speaking tours after that, but by 1892, when George was eighty-eight years old, even he could see that he needed to slow down a little! Although Susannah had taken great care to make the best arrangements she could for them, there were still times when they'd had to travel for six or seven days at a time on a train or spend nights aboard steamships, where they would awake to find rats climbing over them. Despite the hardships, it had been a wonderful seventeen years of traveling. The Müllers had traveled over two hundred thousand miles, visited forty-two countries, and shared the gospel message with people from all manner of background and religious persuasion.

Although George Müller's days of traveling might have been over, his days of useful work were not. With his customary energy, he once again threw himself into the work of the orphanage and the Scriptural Knowledge Institution.

Chapter 16

After Tomorrow...

"George, you must slow down. You aren't as young as you once were!" Susannah Müller looked exasperated.

"None of us are," George replied with a twinkle in his eye. "I'll keep working as long as God gives me the strength to go on."

"I know, but do think about having an afternoon nap. How many other eighty-nine-year-old men do you know who are preaching every Sunday, receiving hundreds of visitors a year, and writing annual reports?"

"Not many," George admitted. "God has blessed me!"

And He had. George Müller considered himself fitter and healthier at eighty-nine than he had been at twenty-nine. He still rose early each morning, dipped his head in icy cold water, and ate a sparse breakfast. And each day he climbed Ashley Down hill to spend the day at his beloved orphanage.

Ironically, it was Susannah Müller, twenty-one years younger than her husband, who died first. Her death was sudden, and so in 1894, George found himself a widower for the second time. George and Susannah had been happily married for twenty-three years, and George missed Susannah greatly.

Since he was alone, George decided it was an unnecessary expense for him to stay in his Paul Street home, where he had lived for over sixty years. It made much more sense for him to move into a room in the Number Three Orphan House, where he could be with the staff and children twenty-four hours a day.

The children loved having George around. They enjoyed it when he wandered into the gardens and asked them questions about their schoolwork or when he told and retold them Bible stories. They also loved the stories he told about the day Queen Victoria was crowned and about the orphanage and the day the orphans moved to Ashley Down from Wilson Street. Many orphans who had grown up in the orphanage were delighted to find George living there when they came to visit. Some of them even brought their grandchildren back to introduce to George. Of course, this really made him feel old!

In the summer of 1897, Queen Victoria celebrated her Diamond Jubilee, making her the longest reigning monarch England had ever had. Yet she was not even queen when George opened the first orphan house on Wilson Street. It was hard for him to believe it had been over sixty years ago. He remembered the opening day as if it were yesterday. He also remembered taking Mary and Lydia and some of the older orphans to the parade in honor of Queen Victoria's coronation. In his mind's eye he could still see the cheering crowds and the delighted looks on the faces of the children. In honor of Queen Victoria's sixty years on the throne, the mayor of Bristol sent fifty pounds from the city's Jubilee Fund to the orphanage for George to use in helping the children celebrate the jubilee. As a result, the older children spent a wonderful day at Clifton Zoo, complete with tea cakes and cold lemonade. And while the older children were gone, the toddlers enjoyed their own nursery party in honor of Queen Victoria.

One Sunday morning, about six months after Queen Victoria's Diamond Jubilee, as George preached his usual sermon at Bethesda Chapel, he spoke of how Jesus is the same yesterday, today, and forever. As he spoke, his face shone. He told the congregation, "I am a happy old man! I walk about my room and say, 'Lord, I am not alone, for You are with me. I have buried my wives and my children, but You are left. I am never lonely or desolate with You and with Your smile, which is better than life!'"

About a month later, on Wednesday, March 9, 1898, George Müller, now ninety-two years old, completed his usual duties at the orphanage. In the afternoon he confessed to Jim Wright that he'd had a little difficulty getting himself dressed that morning. He had become so tired he'd needed to rest three times but, George added, "God is good, and I feel perfectly fine now."

"Perhaps you ought to allow someone to help you dress in the mornings," Jim Wright suggested tactfully. "I'm sure I could arrange it right away."

George thought for a moment. There had been many other times when people suggested he should have a personal assistant. Now, for the first time, he agreed it would soon be necessary. He patted his son-in-law's arm. "After tomorrow, Jim. Send me a helper after tomorrow...."

But tomorrow never came for George Müller. That night George led the prayer meeting at Number Three Orphan House and then went up to his room. He read his Bible for a few minutes. (He had read it through completely over three hundred times since becoming a Christian.) Then he retired to bed. Around five o'clock the next morning, George Müller died peacefully.

By nine o'clock, the whole of Bristol was in an uproar. George Müller, the beloved father to ten thousand orphans, was dead. Bells all over the city tolled, and hundreds of people flocked to the orphanage to pay their respects.

The following Monday, the biggest funeral service in the history of Bristol took place. All of the shops and businesses in the city were closed, and thousands of people lined the streets to catch a glimpse of the funeral procession as it wound its way from Number Three Orphan House to Bethesda Chapel, where the funeral service would be held. As the procession passed Bristol Cathedral, the bells tolled, flags were flown at half-mast, and, as was the custom in Victorian times, the windows in the city were draped with black curtains or were covered with black shutters.

About fifteen hundred orphans, all those who were old enough to walk the distance, marched in rank behind the coach carrying George Müller's coffin. The children were joined by hundreds of men and women who had grown up in the orphanage, including some who had been in the original orphanage on Wilson Street when it opened in 1836.

Thousands of mourners stood quietly outside the church as the funeral service took place. There was no way for them all to fit inside. After a final hymn was sung, the procession made its way from Bethesda Chapel to the cemetery. Over one hundred carriages joined in the procession, including one carrying the mayor of Bristol and his family. Seven thousand people stood respectfully at the cemetery as George Müller was buried under a yew tree between his two wives, Mary and Susannah.

The funeral service was reported all over England, and news of it went out on the telegraph wires around the world. The *Daily Telegraph* wrote that George Müller had "robbed the cruel streets of thousands of victims, the jails of thousands of felons, and the poorhouses of thousands of helpless waifs." And how had he done this? The *Liverpool Mercury* wrote, "How was this wonder accomplished? Mr. Müller has told the world that it was the result of 'Prayer.' The rationalism of the day will sneer at this declaration; but the facts remain."

The *Liverpool Mercury* was right. No matter what anyone thought of George Müller's religious ideas, the facts were amazing. In the sixty-three years he had run the orphanage, he had taken full responsibility for the care of over ten thousand orphaned children.

George Müller had truly learned the lesson of being a good steward of God's money. He went from being a boy who stole from his father and a young man who used whatever means he could to swindle money from his friends to a man God trusted with a fortune, a man who kept so little for himself that when he died, he had only one hundred sixty pounds in his estate, and most of that was the value of a few pieces of furniture.

In his lifetime, nearly one and one-half million pounds passed through George Müller's hands. As well as supporting the orphanage, one hundred fifteen thousand pounds of this money was spent on running Sunday schools and regular schools around the world. Ninety thousand pounds was used for printing and distributing Bibles, and over two hundred sixty thousand pounds went to supporting missionaries. One of the many missionary organizations George gave to was the China Inland

Mission, founded by Hudson Taylor, who had become a good friend. During a particularly difficult period in China, George sent enough money to Hudson Taylor to support all the missionaries of the China Inland Mission!

George Müller was not a man driven by pride or greed. He was a humble man who allowed huge sums of money to pass through his hands. He recognized that it was God's money, not his, and it was to be used in ways that would demonstrate God's love for people. Everything George did was toward furthering that end. As a result, thousands of people's lives were touched and changed. Today the lives of those George touched, as well as the manner in which he lived his own life, are a demonstration to every Christian of the impact a life of simple faith can have.

Chapter 17

The Work Goes On

As George Müller grew older, many people became concerned about what would happen to the orphanage when he died. Some people got up the courage and asked him outright. George always gave the same answer. "When it is the Lord's pleasure to remove this servant from my post, people will see that it is I who was dependent on Him and not He who was dependent on me. He can and will easily raise up another servant, and if he acts in accordance with the principles I have learned and lived, the orphan houses will continue to flourish."

When George Müller died in 1898, many people predicted that the orphanage would die with him. But George's faith proved them wrong. George's son-in-law Jim Wright took over full responsibility for the orphanage. He had in fact been managing its day-to-day operation for quite some time. Under his guidance, the orphanage continued to run as it always had. George Müller's pattern was followed exactly: No one but God was ever asked to supply money to keep it running, and the orphans were always well cared for and well loved.

Over time, however, social conditions began to change. Public health conditions improved so much from the time George Müller first arrived in Bristol that many of the diseases that had routinely claimed the lives of adults became easily treatable. This meant that there were fewer orphans in Great Britain. By the end of World War Two in 1945, only one hundred eighty orphans were living in the huge buildings on Ashley Down. It was decided that these orphans would be better served living in smaller group homes, where they could enjoy more of a family atmosphere. In 1948, the process of selling off the five orphan houses began. The houses were all eventually sold to the Bristol Education Authority to be converted into a Technical Institute. The last orphan left the orphanage on Ashley Down for good in 1958.

The money from the sale of the orphan houses was used to buy many smaller homes throughout Bristol and the surrounding countryside. These homes were known as the Müller Family Homes, in which the orphans lived in more intimate family settings. Some of the money was also used to buy a large home with a beautiful garden. The home was named Müller House and is still used today as the headquarters of the Müller Foundation. Müller House also contains a small museum, along with all the records of the children who were raised in the orphanage.

In the late 1970s, yet another change was made in the way the orphans were cared for. The number of children needing to live in orphanages, even small family-style orphanages, decreased. Since foster homes were seen as a better living situation for these children, the Müller Family Homes were closed down. But this was not the end of the Müller Foundation. The director and staff searched for ways they could still be useful to children in need. Their solution was to open daycare centers and family support centers where parents and children in need could find help.

In 1987, two full-time school workers from the foundation were appointed to work in the local schools in Bristol. Their job was to set up Christian groups within schools and be available to lead religious assemblies for public schools.

Another ministry was also begun that in one sense was the work that George Müller had started come full circle. Beginning in the late twentieth century, it has often been the elderly who have needed more help than orphans. In 1983, the Müller Foundation once again bought property and set up homes, this time for elderly people! Some of these elderly people live permanently at Tranquil House or Tilsley House, while others just come for short stays. Some of the people in these homes are "Müller children," who as orphans grew up at Ashley Down and, after living productive lives, now need a helping hand in their old age.

The work of the Scriptural Knowledge Institution also still goes on. From the beginning, George Müller used money given to him to support many missionaries, including, at times, whole mission organizations. In 1998, one hundred years after George Müller's death, over four hundred thousand pounds was channeled through the Scriptural Knowledge Institution to missionaries serving in mission fields all over the world.

And what of the orphanage buildings themselves? They still stand proudly on Ashley Down, though the city of Bristol has long since grown around them. Today they are part of the University of the West of England. There is a plan to list them as historic sites so that they can be preserved for future generations. Once a year, in September, the university graciously opens up the old Number Three Orphan House to the orphans who once lived there so that they can hold a reunion and thanksgiving service.

While George Müller would probably have liked to have seen the buildings preserved, and while the buildings hold many special memories for thousands of orphans, the buildings were never the focus of George's work. The children were always the focus. George Müller's heart went out to children in need, and George tried to address those needs as best he could, whether by feeding hungry, homeless children in his own home or by ordering five hundred pairs of shoes at a time for the orphans in his care. The buildings were merely a tool in George Müller's ongoing effort to meet the needs of orphan children.

Today, not only is George Müller's work still well known and respected in Bristol, but also over one hundred sixty-five years after George began working with needy children, others still carry on his work in an unbroken chain, praying and striving to meet the needs of children as well as adults.

Bibliography

Bailey, Faith Coxe. *George Müller.* Moody Press, 1958.

Miller, Basil. *George Müller: Man of Faith and Miracles.* Bethany House Publishers, 1941.

Müller, George. *The Autobiography of George Müller.* Whitaker House, 1984.

Steer, Roger. *George Müller: Delighted in God!* Harold Shaw Publishers, 1975.

About the Authors

Janet and Geoff Benge are a husband and wife writing team with more than thirty years of writing experience. Janet is a former elementary school teacher. Geoff holds a degree in history. Originally from New Zealand, the Benges spent ten years serving with Youth With A Mission. They have two daughters, Laura and Shannon, and an adopted son, Lito. They make their home in the Orlando, Florida, area.

Also from Janet and Geoff Benge...

More adventure-filled biographies for ages 10 to 100!

Christian Heroes: Then and Now

Gladys Aylward: The Adventure of a Lifetime • *978-1-57658-019-6*
Nate Saint: On a Wing and a Prayer • *978-1-57658-017-2*
Hudson Taylor: Deep in the Heart of China • *978-1-57658-016-5*
Amy Carmichael: Rescuer of Precious Gems • *978-1-57658-018-9*
Eric Liddell: Something Greater Than Gold • *978-1-57658-137-7*
Corrie ten Boom: Keeper of the Angels' Den • *978-1-57658-136-0*
William Carey: Obliged to Go • *978-1-57658-147-6*
George Müller: Guardian of Bristol's Orphans • *978-1-57658-145-2*
Jim Elliot: One Great Purpose • *978-1-57658-146-9*
Mary Slessor: Forward into Calabar • *978-1-57658-148-3*
David Livingstone: Africa's Trailblazer • *978-1-57658-153-7*
Betty Greene: Wings to Serve • *978-1-57658-152-0*
Adoniram Judson: Bound for Burma • *978-1-57658-161-2*
Cameron Townsend: Good News in Every Language • *978-1-57658-164-3*
Jonathan Goforth: An Open Door in China • *978-1-57658-174-2*
Lottie Moon: Giving Her All for China • *978-1-57658-188-9*
John Williams: Messenger of Peace • *978-1-57658-256-5*
William Booth: Soup, Soap, and Salvation • *978-1-57658-258-9*
Rowland Bingham: Into Africa's Interior • *978-1-57658-282-4*
Ida Scudder: Healing Bodies, Touching Hearts • *978-1-57658-285-5*
Wilfred Grenfell: Fisher of Men • *978-1-57658-292-3*
Lillian Trasher: The Greatest Wonder in Egypt • *978-1-57658-305-0*
Loren Cunningham: Into All the World • *978-1-57658-199-5*
Florence Young: Mission Accomplished • *978-1-57658-313-5*
Sundar Singh: Footprints Over the Mountains • *978-1-57658-318-0*
C.T. Studd: No Retreat • *978-1-57658-288-6*
Rachel Saint: A Star in the Jungle • *978-1-57658-337-1*
Brother Andrew: God's Secret Agent • *978-1-57658-355-5*
Clarence Jones: Mr. Radio • *978-1-57658-343-2*
Count Zinzendorf: Firstfruit • *978-1-57658-262-6*
John Wesley: The World His Parish • *978-1-57658-382-1*
C. S. Lewis: Master Storyteller • *978-1-57658-385-2*
David Bussau: Facing the World Head-on • *978-1-57658-415-6*
Jacob DeShazer: Forgive Your Enemies • *978-1-57658-475-0*
Isobel Kuhn: On the Roof of the World • *978-1-57658-497-2*
Elisabeth Elliot: Joyful Surrender • *978-1-57658-513-9*
D. L. Moody: Bringing Souls to Christ • *978-1-57658-552-8*
Paul Brand: Helping Hands • *978-1-57658-536-8*
Dietrich Bonhoeffer: In the Midst of Wickedness • *978-1-57658-713-3*
Francis Asbury: Circuit Rider • *978-1-57658-737-9*
Samuel Zwemer: The Burden of Arabia • *978-1-57658-738-6*

Klaus-Dieter John: Hope in the Land of the Incas • 978-1-57658-826-2
Mildred Cable: Through the Jade Gate • 978-1-57658-886-4
John Flynn: Into the Never Never • 978-1-57658-898-7
Richard Wurmbrand: Love Your Enemies • 978-1-57658-987-8
Charles Mulli: We Are Family • 978-1-57658-894-9
John Newton: Change of Heart • 978-1-57658-909-0
Helen Roseveare: Mama Luka • 978-1-57658-910-6
Norman Grubb: Mission Builder • 978-1-57658-915-1
Albert Schweitzer: Le Grand Docteur • 978-1-57658-961-8

Heroes of History

George Washington Carver: From Slave to Scientist • 978-1-883002-78-7
Abraham Lincoln: A New Birth of Freedom • 978-1-883002-79-4
Meriwether Lewis: Off the Edge of the Map • 978-1-883002-80-0
George Washington: True Patriot • 978-1-883002-81-7
William Penn: Liberty and Justice for All • 978-1-883002-82-4
Harriet Tubman: Freedombound • 978-1-883002-90-9
John Adams: Independence Forever • 978-1-883002-50-3
Clara Barton: Courage under Fire • 978-1-883002-51-0
Daniel Boone: Frontiersman • 978-1-932096-09-5
Theodore Roosevelt: An American Original • 978-1-932096-10-1
Douglas MacArthur: What Greater Honor • 978-1-932096-15-6
Benjamin Franklin: Live Wire • 978-1-932096-14-9
Christopher Columbus: Across the Ocean Sea • 978-1-932096-23-1
Laura Ingalls Wilder: A Storybook Life • 978-1-932096-32-3
Orville Wright: The Flyer • 978-1-932096-34-7
Captain John Smith: A Foothold in the New World • 978-1-932096-36-1
Thomas Edison: Inspiration and Hard Work • 978-1-932096-37-8
Alan Shepard: Higher and Faster • 978-1-932096-41-5
Ronald Reagan: Destiny at His Side • 978-1-932096-65-1
Davy Crockett: Ever Westward • 978-1-932096-67-5
Milton Hershey: More Than Chocolate • 978-1-932096-82-8
Billy Graham: America's Pastor • 978-1-62486-024-9
Ben Carson: A Chance at Life • 978-1-62486-034-8
Louis Zamperini: Redemption • 978-1-62486-049-2
Elizabeth Fry: Angel of Newgate • 978-1-62486-064-5
William Wilberforce: Take Up the Fight • 978-1-62486-057-7
William Bradford: Plymouth's Rock • 978-1-62486-092-8
Ernest Shackleton: Going South • 978-1-62486-093-5
Benjamin Rush: The Common Good • 978-1-62486-123-9
Dwight Eisenhower: Supreme Commander • 978-1-62486-142-0
Frederick Douglass: The Right to Dignity • 978-1-62486-151-2
Winston Churchill: Resolute • 978-1-62486-153-6

Christian Heroes: Then & Now
GLADYS AYLWARD
The Adventure of a Lifetime
JANET & GEOFF BENGE

Christian Heroes: Then & Now
GLADYS AYLWARD
The Adventure of a Lifetime
JANET & GEOFF BENGE
YWAM

Audio Heroes
Christian Heroes: Then & Now
GLADYS AYLWARD
The Adventure of a Lifetime
JANET & GEOFF BENGE

Christian Heroes: Then & Now
GEORGE MÜLLER
The Guardian of Bristol's Orphans
JANET & GEOFF BENGE

Christian Heroes: Then & Now
GEORGE MÜLLER
The Guardian of Bristol's Orphans
JANET & GEOFF BENGE
YWAM

Audio Heroes
Christian Heroes: Then & Now
GEORGE MÜLLER
The Guardian of Bristol's Orphans
JANET & GEOFF BENGE